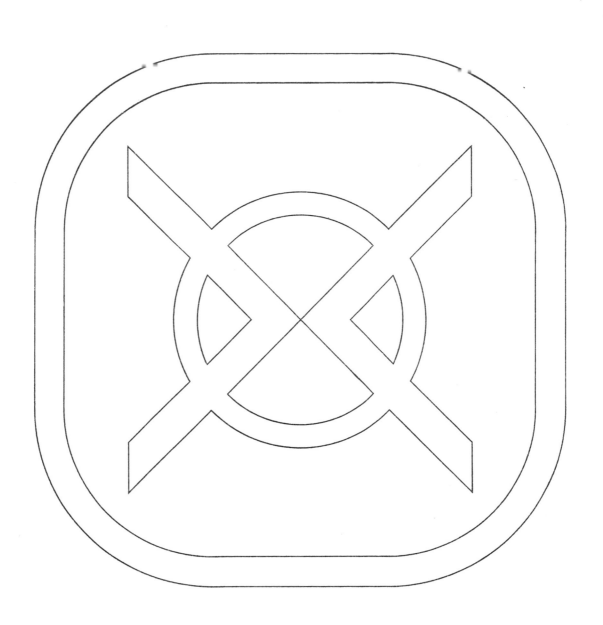

Planning for
industry
art
&
education

as executed by Pieter Brattinga

Greg. Conway.

introduced by
Louis Dorfsman, Vice-President,
Columbia Broadcasting System, New York and
Theo Crosby, Partner,
Crosby, Fletcher & Forbes, London.

Van Nostrand Reinhold Company - New York

Produced in the Netherlands at:
Steendrukkerij de Jong & Co, Hilversum (offset)
Drukkerij Lecturis, Eindhoven (letterpress)
Drukkerij Vada, Wageningen (gravure)
Binderij Sijthoff, Leiden (binding)

Published simultaneously by
Van Nostrand Reinhold Company 450 West 33rd Street, New York, N.Y. 10001 and
A.W.Bruna en Zoon Utrecht
Published in Canada by
D. van Nostrand Company (Canada), Ltd.
16 15 14 13 12 11 10 9 8 7 6 5 4 3 2 1

4

Table of contents:

Acknowledgements

This book contains a great number of photographs and reproductions, most of which have never been published before.

The publishers wish to acknowledge the Japanese initiative by Katsumi Masaru to collect material for this book about Pieter Brattinga who is not only a designer, not only an educator, not only a promoter, but a thinker and planner in the true sense of the word. Introductions to the sections are by Rosamund Howe-Jones who also edited translated material.

The publishers wish to thank the following publishers for their permission to reprint exerpts from previously published material:

De Volkskrant, Amsterdam; Graphic Design, Tokyo; Pagina, Milan; Documentation 1st Biennale of the Poster '66, Warsaw; Stedelijk Museum, Amsterdam; Vista Books, London; Frankfurter Algemeine Zeitung, Frankfurt; De Waarheid, Amsterdam; Algemeen Dagblad, Rotterdam; Het Vrije Volk, Amsterdam; Printing News, London; Nieuwsblad voor de Boekhandel, Amsterdam; Het Parool, Amsterdam; De Haagse Post, Amsterdam; Het Algemeen Handelsblad, Amsterdam; Drukkersweekblad, Amsterdam; Architectural Review, London; De Groene Amsterdammer, Amsterdam; De Gooi- en Eemlander, Hilversum; Newsweek, New York; De Nieuwe Rotterdamsche Courant, Rotterdam; Goois Nieuwsblad, Hilversum; Graphis, Zürich; Vrij Nederland, Amsterdam; L'Architecture d'Aujourd'hui, Paris; Radio en Televisie Weekblad, Bruxelles; Idea, Tokyo; Möbel und Dekoration, Stuttgart; Intergrafia, Amsterdam; Studio, London; De Nieuwe Linie, Amsterdam. Pieter Brattinga made his files available and has been most helpful in checking some dates and facts.

The Publishers.

Perhaps it is because I am accustomed to practising my craft in the U.S.A. where specialization is and has been the order of the day that I find the 'renaissance-man' qualities of Pieter Brattinga most impressive as well as refreshing.

As a design/art/advertising executive within a large and vibrant industry and faced daily with problems where solutions go beyond design, I have an even greater respect for the range and scope of activities that engage his energies and talents.

My first contact with Pieter Brattinga happened more than 15 years ago. My work was exhibited at steendrukkerij de Jong & Co. The unique concept of these ever-changing and most avantgarde exhibits was the brain child of Pieter Brattinga. They were, and still are, far ahead of the times in terms of quality of content, display and exhibit techniques, and manner of promotion.

As I look back at some of them, I can only marvel at their contemporaneousness – right to and beyond this moment in time.

His Quadrat Prints series set new standards in design as well as withstanding the test of time. (Come to think of it, I cannot conjure up a Pieter Brattinga work that has grown old-fashioned). Designer, typographer, printer, thinker, educator, teacher, entrepreneur. Is there any more that one can achieve – and at such a high level of competence and professionalism?

One will find within the cover of this book complete documentation and graphic evidence that what I have just written about Pieter Brattinga is a complete understatement.

Louis Dorfsman

9

It is a cliché that we live in a world of specialists, that in the twentieth century knowledge consists in knowing more and still more about less. It is certainly true that we have around us vast numbers of maimed personalities whose grasp of one subject leaves them entirely incapable of comprehending other specialities. No one can today pretend, as Newton could, to encompass the whole of knowledge, and hardly anyone dares try. And no one can now expect to make fundamental discoveries in any of the major disciplines.

It is also true that conversation, in the 18th century sense of informed discussion, has almost ceased to exist. Instead there is now merely an exchange of specialists' jargon, which generally excites mutual suspicion rather than understanding. Yet at the same time the classical disciplines are fusing together and it is in the relation between the disciplines that most of the best work is now being done, in art as in science. We see a constant interchange between painting, sculpture, poetry, the theatre, between architecture, art and product design. This rich interchange is the result of the example of a few great generalists; promoters and organisers as well as creators, they have, by their grasp of contemporary intellectual concerns, been able to direct those efforts and at the same time make them intelligible. William Morris was perhaps the first to externalize a whole culture, but many others have been extraordinarily influential: Diaghilev, Theo van Doesburg, Walter Gropius, Max Bill, Herbert Read, Tomas Maldonado, Pieter Brattinga.

Brattinga works at the interface of art, communications and education, and like his countryman van Doesburg, is primarily an organizer and promoter, a propagandist.

His basic skill is as a typographer and graphic designer. This is enormous though underrated, mainly because it is always used as a vehicle for something else and never as an end in itself. It is thus an anonymous vehicle for a concept or an idea, or to promote another artist, and not as an advertisement for himself.

In his work for industry the typographer's skills, clarity, precision and thoroughness, are uppermost. He can define a brief, produce a concept, or find the right person for a job.

In the exhibitions at the De Jong printing works, and in the famous Quadrat Prints he has made a wide impact on the world's art scene. Many of the exhibitions, though on a small scale, have been truly seminal: the first showing of many artists now considered important; of things previously invisible suddenly made manifest, such as street signs and manhole covers; and above all the creative exploration of the exhibition medium as an end in itself. These latter, the exhibition of smells, the opening of the show of artificial food and many others were early Happenings, demanding participation and involvement from the audience. More important, they are always occasions, well publicized and promoted to gain a maximum impact.

The Quadrat Prints, too, have been used to promote or encourage many artists and they act also as a vehicle for artistic or typographic experiment, by the artists concerned. They are always superbly produced (as publicity material for De Jong) and constitute a marvellous promotional idea for the firm, enlightened and generous, yet commercially soundly based. It is this intelligent double motive that characterizes much of Brattinga's thinking.

To the public he is a creator of exhibitions, sometimes on a very large scale. The exhibitions are always total, the layout, catalogues, posters are all concentrated on the idea of communication, in service to the artist and his works. He is also an apologist for modern art. A critic is seldom capable of artistic creation, but Brattinga writes and talks with wit and a sense of amused participation in the process, because he is involved and committed.

These preoccupations have led naturally to his involvement in education, as a teacher and inevitably as an organiser of courses. The stints at the Pratt Institute in New York and at other design institutions around the world have given him great experience, and opportunities to influence a whole generation of designers.

Of course, he has been lucky. To be the son of a printing press owner is to start well ahead in the communications game, but Brattinga has taken it from there in remarkable style. The list of his activities reads like a catalogue of the avantgarde of the past 10 years. And of course, it helps to be Dutch, to be born into a tight, civilized, comprehensible country, in a tradition of frugality, work, precision and order. A great part of that tradition is outward looking and exploratory, and Brattinga has made himself part of it.

Theo Crosby

The Mediator, Simon Vinkenoog

The man who objectively follows and records the course of many events for the sole purpose of benefiting himself and his fellow-men is a new type of human being: he acts as a communication expert, or mediator between people and groups, between interests and needs. A new human being who helps to shape the future by taking a positive constructive part in building the present. It is not merely a matter of efficiency – although the release of manpower implies the possibility of using human intellect elsewhere in creating new projects.

Contact need not be difficult; any intelligent scientist knows how to communicate with another about a given problem – which is no problem in a different frame of reference, or which may cease to be one owing to some recent development.

The mediator 'surmises' because he has specialized in gathering knowledge transcending all disciplines and enabling him to gain insight from everyday practice; thanks to observation and operational research his conjectures can be verified. For is not whatever he finds open to inspection by anyone who may be interested?

The mediator often succeeds in re-establishing, restoring a long-lost contact. The creative power he must possess enables him to suggest such solutions as come to his mind through his sense of responsibility and his involvement. His is the view of an outsider within a given structure, a routine, a machine, a setup – and his practised eye recognizes, because it sees for the first time, the flaws escaping those who have grow nused to them day by day without being capable of tracing them to their source. The mediator resolves conflicts, not as a physician – although he derives much from physiology and psychology and although, like the physician, he can test his theories in actual practice. He is uncommitted, he does not represent any organization, and is only obliged to choose when offered the opportunity of examining all aspects of a given problem. He is without bias, unless it is a question of taking action – any action – against stagnancy in the form of apathy, fear, short - sightedness. Much work is done at cross-purposes; much energy is wasted because men pore over problems that have already been solved.

When someone else describes what is happening within us, does it not become clear what cripples the inner man in finding his true projection? He who wants to know everything inherits the future – the mediator is the man who gives shape to his curiosity by being alert to whatever he may still be able to accomplish.

He does not sit back and wait, but keeps knocking on the door. His speech is direct, and confined to essentials. He penetrates to the core of things and does not let himself be taken in by appearances.

He says: what I like best is to work out ideas; mankind has them by the myriad waiting to be picked up and used. When we come together there is bound to be mutual inspiration.

These words belong to all men. In all of them I have a rightful share. Thinking man finally meets his ilk on the plane of dialogue, each partner in his own way establishing a basis in the concept of synthesis emerging from the clash of thesis and anti-thesis.

How many potent hypotheses are lying dormant in each man's professional literature; how many unfulfilled wishes, unsatisfied desires? How much careful study have others undertaken for us in the shape of pilot projects, calculations and proposals, not least in respect of the co-operative phenomena that were inconceivable in past centuries and that have not even penetrated the minds of many of our contemporaries? Friends recognized in those with whom we are able to collaborate effectively within the existing social forms are friends for ever. He who is his own master has no need for public relations, image or status – behind the mask, the façade, objectivity lies hidden and it can be freed by everyone and for everyone through an intelligent approach.

Man is involved in a laborious process of evolution and in our age he is no longer required (like Disraeli in Parliament) to choose between ape and angel. He has reached a stage where he can focus on the question of his essence.

Man is faced with the crucial alternative: assuming greater responsibility in exercising his duties by breaking away from his own limits, or accepting the status quo, which sets up barriers among us and so perpetuates artificial differences. Within this broad context the mediator stands uncommitted: he is constantly on the way, his world expands day after new day.

The fewer illusions, the greater the power to act, and the more signposts pointing a way out of seemingly insoluble problems. The more insistent the appeal to take simple decisions, the wider the mental horizon. Reaching out beyond himself man may in the end achieve anything; he is his own arbiter: only self-imposed obstacles can stop him on the road to fulfilment. Every day brings

new falicities, inventions, experiments, ideas: and ideas do not let themselves be confined within the categories we know at present. Each new idea always represents an extra dimension.
By trying it out in practice, by exploring the lately discovered ground we are able to secure the manpower, the time, the energy, the matter we want to invest in the future.

'Proeve van Kommunikatie, Form Mediation International', Amsterdam, Netherlands 1967.

Czech and Polish awards for Dutch graphic designers, Lidy van Marissing

This summer three Dutch artists have won prizes in an Eastern European country. At the Third
Biennial Festival of Graphic Arts held at Brno (Czechoslovakia), Pieter Brattinga was given the
highest award – The Grand Prize – for his contribution to the international show of exhibition
designs.
Brattinga sent in photographs of shows he had designed or directed during the past 15 years: an
instructional exhibition of the New York Pratt Institute (which took place during his stay in the
United States from 1960 to 1964) and about thirty exhibitions held at steendrukkerij de Jong & Co
in Hilversum, Holland. Among them were the first one-man exhibitions of work by Sandberg,
Carel Visser, Tajiri, Piet Zwart, and Fritzi ten Harmsen van Beek.
Brattinga, who started out as a graphic designer, devotes most of his time to his firm, which bears
the intriguing name of Form Mediation International. Although he is averse to being given a label
of any kind, he might be best defined as a mediator between art and capital.
'An industrialist doesn't know what to ask of an artist, how to put across what's on his mind',
says Brattinga. 'He speaks a different language from the artist's. The world is turning into a
collection of specialists who have little left to say to one another except 'How are you?' They lack
the vocabulary and the interest to get beyond that point. People are no longer able to talk to each
other without lapsing into professional jargon. In the States it's even worse than in Europe. I'm a
mediator between two specialized groups'.
'Each problem needs its own specific approach. It's very strenuous work, actually. The advice you
give must still be valid in five years' time. This job keeps you constantly on your toes. I see seven
national papers plus some foreign ones every day. I have to read magazines ranging from Fortune
(for the industrialist) to Art International (for the artist); from publications of the Werkgroep 2000
(a study group of Futurologists) to scientific journals'.
At least once a year Brattinga designs a poster for the Kröller-Müller Museum (an important
museum of modern art and sculpture located in central Holland). He made both catalogue and
poster for the Henry Moore exhibition held there in 1968, and the open-design poster for the
exhibition 'The Silence of Motion' which took place at the museum in 1967. The striking catalogue
for Carel Visser, the Dutchman at the Venice Biennale, was also his work.
At regular intervals he also designs posters for steendrukkerij de Jong. Says he: 'It's all very well
to theorize, but that shouldn't stop you from dirtying your hands every now and then'.

De Volkskrant, Amsterdam, Netherlands; August 9th, 1968.

Planning for industry

Planning for industry

Planning for industry is based on an analysis of industry itself. Every self-respecting industry should have a 3 or 5 year plan, or at least a goal towards which they are working. Without a plan, work proceeds in total uncertainty. An organization must know not only that they intend to make money but how, and with what.
Every successful industry must have an image, and that will depend on their communication with their public. In each case the public will be different: a railway company will have a general public, a drug firm will have a medically conscious public. Brattinga's specialization is to plan this communication. Knowing about future developments in the field of visual communications, knowing what architects, musicians and other artists are available to give form to ideas which are alive in industry, enables him to help industry to plan their advertising, indicate the direction in which they are travelling.

D.S.M.

D.S.M. (Dutch State Mines), originally a mining organization, is now a large chemical company with branches scattered throughout the Netherlands.
In 1966, Brattinga was asked to coordinate and standardize the various aspects of visual design in the industry as a whole. Apart from producing a unified and consistent image for the company it was intended that the scheme should also be economically beneficial. Often standardization within an organization can lead to a reduction in the number of different items needed and a streamlining of production procedures. This in turn reduces costs.
Brattinga's first step was to form a committee made up of members from the different departments connected with the problems being studied, departments which previously had often worked at cross-purposes owing to lack of communication. The committee') began by listing all items which helped to form the image of D.S.M., from the trademark, letterheads, safety signs and colours, container labels, right through to the signs on the railway carriages used by the company. Working systematically, they compiled what Brattinga believes to be the most advanced design manual in the world.

Every aspect of design in the company is covered by the manual. After research a typeface was chosen and grid systems were developed for promotional publications, correspondence paper used both internally and externally, and for forms. This not only gave a distinct style which could become identified with D.S.M. but in the case of forms also resulted in time being saved because the design allowed the typist to insert data more quickly. For all published material instructions were laid down for composing, for the use of colour, and directions were given to the author on points of editorial procedure. Guidelines for photographers and artists were also included. A functional colour code was devised to indicate groups of chemicals, also a safety colour code for potentially dangerous substances. Because the systems were adopted throughout the company, an employee transferred from one department to another would encounter familiar colour signs and symbols in his new job. Signs used both inside and outside factory premises were standardized in respect to colour, lettering, placing and use of material. Substantial savings were made by replacing hand-painted cardboard signs with a life of 2 years, by aluminium signs that could be used for 15 years.
These are some examples of items included in the manual, parts of which are reproduced on the following pages.

Different, Dick Dooijes

... It is the impressive approach to the reform of the visual aspect of what until recently was known as the Staatsmijnen and what is now called DSM. A working party, guided by Pieter Brattinga but composed of employees of the gigantic enterprise has studied this matter thoroughly since 1966 and on December 3rd last has published the results of its activities ...
... What has been evolved here by a team in close and prolonged co-operation possesses many aspects worth taking note of. I was particularly struck by the fine graphic presentation of the various elements, which conforms to high esthetic standards. For instance, I consider the new trademark eminently successful in its simplicity. Thus I feel much appreciation of what has been accomplished, yet during the press conference of DSM I could not resist the urge to ask with regard to this subject whether in future there would be any room left for the startling, personal whim of an individual designer.

'Drukkerswereld', Amsterdam, Netherlands; January 2nd, 1970

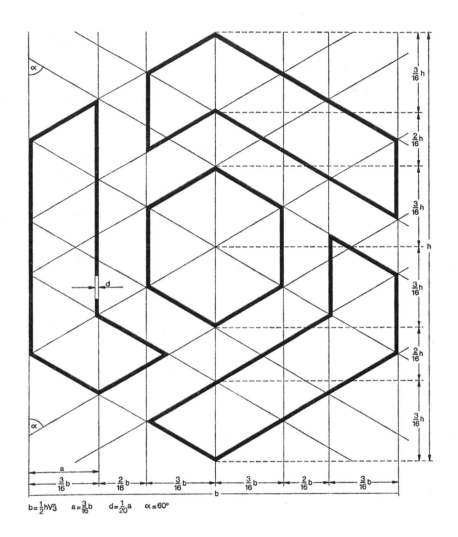

$$b = \tfrac{1}{2}h\sqrt{3} \qquad a = \tfrac{3}{16}b \qquad d = \tfrac{1}{20}a \qquad \alpha = 60°$$

Indien het algemeen handelsmerk wordt uitgevoerd in positief (zwart op wit, grijs of geel), worden in deze constructietekening de vier delen waaruit het merk bestaat, zwart opgevuld. De lijndikte d (1/20 van de breedte a) maakt dan deel uit van het merk.
Wordt het algemeen handelsmerk in diapositief uitgevoerd, dan wel aangebracht in wit op zwarte, grijze of gekleurde onder-

grond (behalve geel), dan wordt in deze constructietekening de achtergrond zwart opgevuld, zodat de lijndikte d dan deel uitmaakt van de achtergrond en het merk zelf wordt afgeslankt. Hierdoor ontstaat een optisch gelijke indruk van positief en diapositief merk.
Deze werkwijze voor diapositief wordt gevolgd voor gebruik van het algemeen handelsmerk

bij een hoogte van het merk van meer dan 18 mm, d.w.z. in combinatie met 'DSM' – al of niet met toevoeging van 'Holland' – in een corps groter dan 36 pt. Ook de letters van 'DSM' en 'Holland' worden dan afgeslankt (zie blad 4b. 1, onder Diapositief).
Bij 'DSM' (+ 'Holland') in corpsen tot 36 pt kan het positieve merk (samen met de letters) zonder meer worden omgekeerd.

Novivorm DSM

**Hoofdstuk 15
Tekens, Symbolen, Signalen
f. Beeldborden**

**Blad 15f. 2
december 1969**

Algemeen

Algemeen (401 t/m 450)
401. richtingpijl
402. ingang
403. uitgang
404. bedrijfsgeneeskundige dienst
405. telefoon voor algemeen gebruik
406. postkamer
407. bibliotheek
408. garderobe
409. kantine
410. WC
411. damestoilet
412. herentoilet
413. personenlift

401

402

403

404

405

406

407

408

409

410

411

412

413

Novivorm DSM

Hoofdstuk 13
Tekstborden, Wegwijzers
b. Wegwijzers in openbaar verkeer

Voorbeelden
Constructie pijl

Blad 13b. 2
december 1969

240

← **Stikstofbindingsbedrijf**

← **Organische Fabrieken**

← **Centraal Laboratorium**

Havenbedrijf →

Polychemiebedrijf →

1670

← **Spoorweg- en Expeditiebedrijf**

← **Haven-bedrijf**

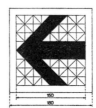

150
180

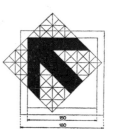

150
180

VARA

In the Netherlands, radio and television transmitting time is divided up between several broadcasting companies. Time allocated to each company is proportional to the membership of the organization, and in practice this is calculated from the number of people subscribing to the broadcasting guide which each company publishes. For this reason competition between the various TV and radio guides is intense and much thought is devoted to their planning.

In 1965, Brattinga was invited to redesign the guide for the **VARA**, one of the biggest broadcasting companies in Holland. Taking the width of the contractual printing press as a fixed point of departure, he experimented with various ways of folding the sheet to arrive at the format which best fitted his method of listing programmes. One system he tried gave the programmes on all channels in one column, listing them in chronological order from the time they began. This called for a long narrow page format. Another method divided the programmes according to their channels, keeping programmes at corresponding times on a level with each other. The page format best suited to this system was short and wide. This scheme resulted in blank spaces being left on the page when the programme on one channel lasted the same length of time as several shorter programmes on another channel. This was an advantage as illustrations could be incorporated to give a pleasing

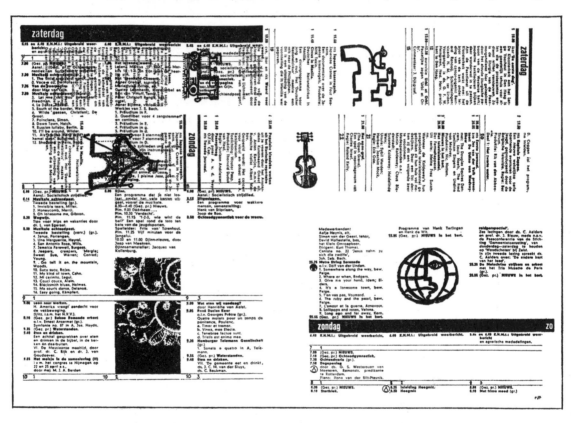

←————————————————— width —————————————————→

22

zaterdag

19.00 ikor 'De eerste dag'.
De Kloosterkerk aan het Lange Voorhout in Den Haag is een geestelijk tehuis voor allen die de protestantse eredienst willen vernieuwen. Zo is de liturgie van de Passiemorgendienst hier geïnspireerd door het aloude liturgische patroon van de Westerse kerk; moderne kerkliederen blijken daar wonderwel in te passen. Aan de Paasdienst uit de Kloosterkerk werkt mee: het koor van de kerk onder leiding van cenor-organist Bernard Renooij. Schitteltzingen: vicaris N. M. A. ter Linden. Voorganger is ds. G. F. W.

12

12.00—12.35 eurovisie Urbi et Orbi. Pauselijke zegen 'Urbi et Orbi'. Commentaar: J. Dijkgraaf.

15

15.90 nts Japanse kraanvogels. Japanese Cranes in Four Seasons. Een documentaire over de Japanse kraanvogels. Produktie: NHK Tokio.

19.40 Circus in Manilla. Deutscher Nationalzirkus in Manilla. Een circusprogramma voor jong en oud. Het 'Deutscher Nationalzirkus' maakte een reis naar de Philippijnen. Dit is een uitzending van de voorstelling die in Manilla werd gegeven.

19

19.00 cvk, ikor en rkk Woord voor weerd. De bijbelvertelling voor de kleuters, geschreven door Mies Bouhuys en geïllustreerd door Bert Bouman. Vertelster: Cecilia Lichtveld. 'Naar het land van morgen'.

19.06 nts Kentucky Jones. Wilde kattensoep (Wild cat soup). Jim denkt Kentucky moedig te kunnen maken door hem een bordje 'Wilde kattensoep' te laten eten. Kentucky Jones: Denis Weaver; Ike Wong: Ricky Der; Seldom Jackson: Harry Morgen. Als gast treedt op: James Dawson.

19.30 cvk-ikor 'De wereld houdt op adem'. In één van de grote middeleeuwse kathedralen van Noord Europa — de kathedraal van York — hebben alle koren van de stad zich verzameld om Passiliederen te zingen. Het orgel wordt bespeeld door de koorleider-dr. Francis Jackson met medewerking van een deel van het BBC Northern Orchestra, onder leiding van Stanford Robinson. Gezongen worden o.a.: Bachs 'Jesu, joy of man's desiring', 'This joyful Eastertide' en het 'Hallelujah' - uit Handel's 'Messiah'. De aartsbisschop van York, dr.

D. Coggan zal het programma inleiden.

2 17.30 nts Kapitein Zeppos. Een nieuwe wekelijkse serie spannende avonturen voor de jeugd, geproduceerd door de Belgische Televisie. Regie: Ber Struys. Produktie: Nic. van den Abbeele. Deel 1: Het zwarte water.

20

2 20.00 nts Eerste Journaal.

2 20.05 kro Jos van der Valk presenteert De Udine van Medvey Show met: The Douglas Squires Dancers, Louis Neefs, The Fred Tomlinson Singers en Undine von Medvey. Produktie: Nic. Notten. Nieuws in het kort.

20.50 Der Fernsehapparat. Uit serie: Meine Frau Susanne. Wanneer de Koldewey's hun paaskracht televisietoestel gebruiken zit hun huis vol medekijkers. Door een list genoegen de list van een volgende keer te beperken. Medespelenden o.a.: Martin Koldewey: Claus Biederstadt; Susanne Koldewey: Heidelinde Weis; Ursula: Sybil Werden; Herbert: Joachim Mock. Regie: Erik Ode.

21

1 21.05 Het open graf. (The Open Grave). Een spel in reportagevorm van Charles Israel. Regie: Roland Kelly.

22

22.00 Populaire klassieke werken uit het Slavische repertoire uit te voeren door het Amsterdams Kunstmaand Orkest o.l.v. Anton Kersjes, m.m.v. de Russische violist Albert Merkov. Gespeeld wordt: Het concert voor viool en orkest van A. Katsjaturian. Toelichting: Wouter Paap. Produktie: Thorvald Dudok van Heel. Regie: Jurriaan Andriessen.

22.40 Paasploeg door pater A. v. d. Weyer O.F.M. Cap.

22.50 nts Tweede Journaal.

zondag

15.00 nts Japanse kraanvogels. Japanese Cranes in Four Seasons. Een documentaire over de Japanse kraanvogels. Produktie: NHK Tokio.

15.40 Circus in Manilla. Deutscher Nationalzirkus in Manilla. Een circusprogramma voor jong en oud. Het 'Deutscher Nationalzirkus' maakte een reis naar de Philippijnen. Dit is een uitzending van de voorstelling die in Manilla werd gegeven.

Medewerkenden: Aafje Heynis, alt; Simon van der Geest, tenor; David Hollestelle, bas; het Klein Omroepkoor. Dirigent: Kurt Thomas. Cantate no. 22 'Jesus nahm zu sich die zwölfe'. Joh. Seb. Bach.

Programma van Henk Terlingen en Henk de Wit.

15.55 (Gez. pr.) NIEUWS in het kort.

15.25 Metro String Serenade o.l.v. Dolf van der Linden.
1. Somewhere along the way, bew. Paige.
2. Where or when, Rodgers.
3. Give me your hand, idem; Elders.
4. It's a lonesome town, bew. Paige.
5. T'en vas pas, Voumard.
6. The ruby and the pearl, bew. Paige.
7. L'amour et la guerre, Aznavour.
8. Lollipops and roses, Velona.
9. Long ago and far away, Kern, Paige.

15.45 (Gez. pr.) NIEUWS in het kort.

reidperspectief. Zes lezingen door ds. C. Aalders en prof. dr. J. Bleuw, mede n.a.v. de Paasconferentie van de Stichting 'Gemeenteopbouw', van donderdag—zaterdag te houden op 'Woudschoten' bij Zeist. In zijn tweede lezing spreekt ds. C. Aalders over: 'De andere kant van het leed'.

22.35 De Molochins strijkers en orkest met het Trio Musette de Paris (gr.).

23.55 (Gez. pr.) NIEUWS in het kort.

zondag ZO

bericht en agrarische mededelingen.

7
7.00 (Gez. pr.) NIEUWS.
7.15 (Gez. pr.) Ochtendgymnastiek.
7.30 Ochtendwrijk (gr.).
7.35 Dagopening door ds. G. S. Westerouen van Meeteren. Remonstr. predikante te Rotterdam. Piano: Ilona van der Bilt-Ptasnik.

8
8.00 (Gez. pr.) NIEUWS.
8.10 Sterrblad.

8.20 Inleiding Hoogmis.
8.25 Hoogmis.

8.40 (Gez. pr.) NIEUWS.
8.15 Met frisse moed (gr.).

P-39-

effect. A system of identifying signs was also devised so that listeners and viewers could easily find programmes of special interest to them. For example, women's broadcasts and sport programmes each had an easily recognizable symbol.[2])
Due to the biggest broadcasting companies deciding to combine their advertisement acquisitioning departments, a new format agreeable to all parties had to be found. The one finally adopted incorporated some of the details of designs developed earlier.[3])

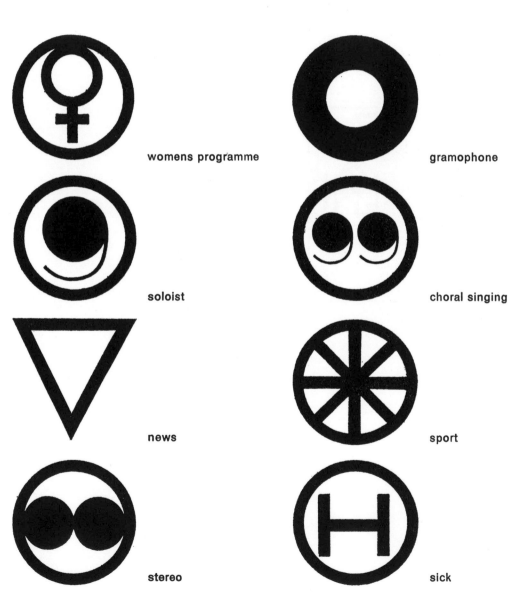

womens programme

gramophone

soloist

choral singing

news

sport

stereo

sick

Hilversum 1 402 m / 746 kHz

●VARA

6.40 KNMI-Weerbericht.

7.00 Nieuwsberichten.
Aansluitend: ochtendgymnastiek.

7.20 Socialistisch strijdlied.

7.23 Uitgeslapen.
Een ontspannen programma voor mensen, samengesteld door Henk van Stipriaan en Nico de Haan.

7.30 Van de voorpagina
door Cor van de Poel.

7.35 Uitgeslapen (vervolg).

VPRO

7.54 Deze dag,
Maria de Groot.

● VARA

8.00 Nieuwsberichten.

8.11 Dingen van de dag.

8.20 Uitgeslapen (vervolg).

9.00 [STEREO] Moskou's kamerorkest o.l.v.
Rudolph Barsjaj.
Orkestsuite nr. 1 in C, BWV 1066,
Joh. Seb. Bach.

9.35 Waterstanden.

9.40 [STEREO] Carl Maria von Weber.
Fagotconcert in F, op. 75. Paul Hongne, fagot, l'Oiseau Lyre Instrumental Ensemble o.l.v. Louis de Froment.

10.00 Terwijl de was droogt
zorgt Teddy Scholten voor een ontspannend plaatje en praatje en kunt u even uitblazen.

NRU

11.00 Nieuwsberichten.

11.02 Premières door de Nederlandse radio-orkesten.
1. In pompa magna, Jurriaan Andriessen. Omroeporkest o.l.v. Roberto Benzi.
2. Serenade per orchestra d'archi e trio di fiato, Van Hemel. Kamerorkest o.l.v. Henk Spruit, m.m.v. Trio di Fiati.
3. Torenmuziek Ommaggio à Sweelinck, Franken. Solist – Piet Bakker, beiaard. Omroeporkest o.l.v. Roelof Krol.
4. Divertimento voor blazers, Bonsel. Kamerorkest o.l.v. Willem van Otterloo.
Samenstelling – Hans Tuijten.

VPRO

12.00 Blauwe maandag.
Met regionale informatie, reportages, mensen achter de feiten, platen.
Samenstelling en presentatie – Erik Boshuijzen.

12.26 Mededelingen voor land- en tuinbouw.

12.29 [STEREO] Muzikale aanwinsten.
Samenstelling – Jan de Kruyff en Han Reiziger.

12.50 Tien voor één.
De heer W. F. H. Hensen.

13.00 Nieuwsberichten.

13.11 Informatie.
Ontwikkelingswerk.
Redactie – Philippe Scheltema.

13.20 Pro memorie.
Redactie – Hans Paardekooper.

13.25 Klassiek decor.
Nederlandse muziekdagen 1966. Het Haarlems Jeugdorkest o.l.v. André Kaart m.m.v. het Vossiuskoor, Marion Mosler en Werner Herbers, hobo.
1. Zes adagio's, Pijper.
2. Hymne Temporum Diei, Van Beurden.
3. 'Concert voor 2 hobo's en orkest, Voormolen.
4. Music for statuseekers, Kox.
(Herhaling van 30-9-1966.)

40

14.25 Schoolradio.
1. Nederland - Waterland.
Muziekspel samengesteld door Bernard van Beurden en Frits Kokkes.
2. Actualiteiten door Kees van Maasdam.

NRU

14.45 Kleintje cabaret.
Samenstelling – Erik van ...

AVRO

15.00 Avrodite.
Een programma voor de vrouw.

15.40 [STEREO] Het orkest Willy Schobben.

16.00 Nieuwsberichten.

16.02 [STEREO] De wereld van de opera.
Beschouwingen over de opera's aan de hand van nieuw verschenen grammofoonplatenopnamen, door Otto Hamburg.
La Gioconda, Ponchielli.
La Gioconda, een straatzangeres – Renata Tebaldi, sopraan,
La Cieca, haar blinde moeder – Oralia Dominguez, alt,
Barnaba, een spion – Robert Merrill, bariton,
Alvise Badoero, een Venetiaans edelman – Nicolai Ghiuselev, bas,
Laura, zijn vrouw – Marilyn Horne, mezzosopraan,
Enzo Grimaldo, verdreven prins van Santa Flor – Carlo Bergonzi, tenor,
Zuane, een gondelier – Silvio Maionica, bas,
Isepo, een schrijver – Piero di Palma, tenor,
een monnik – Silvio Maionica, bas.
Koor en orkest van de Accademia di Santa Cecilia, Rome.
Dirigent – Lamberto Gardelli.

OV

17.45 Den Haag aan de lijn.

AVRO

18.00 Nieuwsberichten.

18.16 Radiojournaal.

18.30 De tafel van (half) zeven.
Een van alles en nog wat programma met als vaste punten:
Thon Rees met zijn rubriek Al wat menselijk is.
Het klokje van zeven uur . . .
en dus en om
19.08 Paris vous parle door Jan Brusse.
Vandaag met tafelmuziek door het ensemble Fred van Ingen.
Presentatie – John van Lier.
Samenstelling – Kees de Wolf.

RVU

19.35 Muzikaal spectrum
door Klaas A. Posthuma.

NRU

20.05 Scala internationaal.
Een maandelijkse round-up van literatuur, toneel, muziek, dans, beeldende kunst en film uit alle delen van de wereld.
Redactie – Pieter Brattinga, Frans van Mastrigt, Henk Romeijn Meijer en Edu Verhulst.

22.30 Nieuwsberichten.

22.40 Actualiteiten.

22.55 Jazzpresso.
Pete Felleman presenteert jazzplaten met kort commentaar onder het motto: Something old, plenty new, nothing borrowed, often blue.

23.25 Radiorama.
Minimagazine met een speciaal nummer.
Samenstelling – Jan Blokker.
Medewerkers – Heleen van Meurs en Philip Bloemendaal.
Produktie en regie – Bob Uschi.

23.55 Nieuwsberichten.

24.00 Sluiting.

Hilversum 2 298 m / 1007 kHz

KRO

5.45 en 6.40 KNMI-Weerbericht.

7.00 Nieuwsberichten.

7.10 Het levende woord.

7.15 Badinerie.
Klassieke grammofoonmuziek.

7.30 Nieuwsberichten.

7.32 Echo.
Weerklank van het dagelijks gebeuren.

7.40 Badinerie.
Klassieke grammofoonmuziek.

7.55 Overweging
door pater J. de Rooy sj.

8.00 Nieuwsberichten.

8.10 Badinerie.
Klassieke grammofoonmuziek.

8.30 Nieuwsberichten.

8.32 Moeders wil is wet.
Verzoekplatenprogramma.

NRU

10.00 Het muziekleven in Nederland van vóór 1940.
Redactie – Rutger Schoute en Willem Strietman.
Het muziekleven in Utrecht, met een speciale belichting van de Evert Cornelis-periode.

11.00 Nieuwsberichten.

KRO

11.02 De zonnebloem.
Radioziekenbezoek o.l.v. Alex van Wayenburg.

11.30 Tussen pisp en stok.
Informatief programma van, door en voor bejaarden.
Presentatie – Fons Disch.
Samenstelling en produktie – Mia Smelt.

NCRV

12.00 Zuidamerikaanse klanken
door de orkesten van Edmundo Ros en Stanley Black (gr.pl.).

12.21 Voor boer en tuinder.

12.26 Mededelingen voor land- en tuinbouw.

12.30 Nieuwsberichten.

Pieter Brattinga werkt mee aan Scala internationaal. 20.05 uur. Hilversum 1.

Renata Tebaldi zingt uit La Gioconda van Ponchielli. 16.02 uur. Hilversum 1.

12.41 Hier en nu.
Actualiteitenrubriek.

12.50 Variant.
Radionelbuffet.

13.30 [STEREO] Orkest Bobby Gutesha.

13.50 Schoolradio.
Voordragen (1).
In deze serie wordt aan de hand van voorbeelden duidelijk gemaakt welke mogelijkheden er zijn om de voordracht van poëzie en proza te verlevendigen.
Medewerking verleenden mevrouw Greet Konings en o.a. leerlingen van de Chr. Kweekschool in Gorinchem.
Samenstelling en presentatie – Elly den Haring.

14.15 Opera (gr.pl.).
Nederlandse solisten.
1. Uit Les contes d'Hoffmann, Offenbach.
Gré Brouwenstijn, sopraan en Lidy van der Veen, mezzosopraan.
Het Nederlands Operakoor en het Radio Filharmonisch orkest o.l.v. Paul van Kempen.
2. Uit Lakmé, Délibes.
Wilma Driessen, sopraan met orkest o.l.v. Pietro Cordone.
3. Uit Zar und Zimmermann, Lortzing.
Marco Bakker, bariton. Iramac Symfonieorkest o.l.v. Leo Driehuys.
4. Uit Cavalleria rusticana, Mascagni.
Marijke van der Lugt, sopraan en het Amsterdams Operakoor.
Het omroeporkest o.l.v. Willem Lohof.
5. Uit Le postillon de Lonjumeau, Adam. John van Kesteren, tenor met het RIAS-koor en het Radiosymfonieorkest o.l.v. Reinhard Peters.
6. Uit Rigoletto, Verdi.
Ans Philippo, sopraan.
Marco Bakker, bariton.
Omroeporkest o.l.v. Roberto Benzi.

15.00 Middagdienst
te leiden door majoor D. Th. Krommenhoek.

NRU

15.30 Zoeklicht op Nederland.
Muziek – Joop de Roo.
Produktie – Maarten Nederhorst.
Samenstelling en regie – Chiel de Kruijf.
Met om:
15.30 Informatie over Utrecht, afgewisseld met muziek.

16.00 Nieuwsberichten.

16.02 Zoeklicht op Nederland (vervolg).
Met om:
16.02 Zoeklicht op andere provincies,. waarbij de correspondenten aan het woord komen.
16.40 Utrechts namiddagconcert.

OV

17.20 Mauricius als dichter in Suriname.
Spreker – F. J. van Wel.

NCRV

17.30 't Kleuterklokje klingelt.

17.45 Maarten.
Een verhaal voor de kleuters geschreven door Jaap ter Haar.
Rolverdeling:
voddeman – Tonny Foletta,
moeder – Corry v. d. Linden,
agent – Han König,
oud vrouwtje – Dogi Rugani,
kinderen – Gerrie Mantel, Martin Simonis, Nina Bergsma.
Regie – Wim Paauw.

18.00 [STEREO] Sweet Sixteen o.l.v.
Lex Karsemeyer
met begeleiding van het Sextet Jo Bos.
1. Pak wat zonnestralen. 2. Come home. 3. A voice in the wilderness.
4. Side saddle. 5. Felicidad.
6. Eenzaam. 7. Colour my world.

Different designs for industry

Aside from being a consultant to industry, Brattinga is also very active as a designer.
A number of logos were designed by him: Page 27: top left; trademark for Form Mediation,
International. top right; logo for an Amsterdam art gallery specializing in multiples.
middle; a trademark for an oil company. top bottom; logo for the office of the Netherlands
National Tourist Office in New York. bottom; a symbol for a marketing and research
institute. Page 26: below; a number of commemorative postage stamps for the celebration of
the 15th anniversary of the Statute for the Kingdom of the Netherlands.

seriaal
seriaal
seriaal
seriaal
seriaal

HOT

NETHERLANDS
NATIONAL TOURIST OFFICE

intomart □□☒

Steendrukkerij de Jong & Co

Design policy of Steendrukkerij de Jong & Co, Katsumi, Masaki

No doubt the consistent use of square shapes was also due to Brattinga's ideas. On every occasion, quadrat shapes were used, whether in pay envelopes, posters or calendars. No doubt, this utilization of square shapes was caused not only by a desire to put across a consistent image, but also by such considerations as economy in the use of paper.
When Brattinga utilized to the full his knowledge and sensitivity in graphic design, functioning as an art director in the true sense of the term, a througgoing design policy was established.
Finally, Brattinga's utilization of square shapes resulted in the goodwill publication known as Quadrat Prints (meaning 'square-shaped prints'), which have been appearing since 1955.

'Graphic Design' number 8, Tokyo, Japan; 1962

z	m	d	w	d	v	z
augustus 27	28	29	30	31	1	2
3	4	5	6	7	8	9
10	11	12	13	14	15	16
17	18	19	20	21	22	23
24	25	26	27	28	29	30
31	1	2	3	4	5	6
7	8	9	10	11	12	13

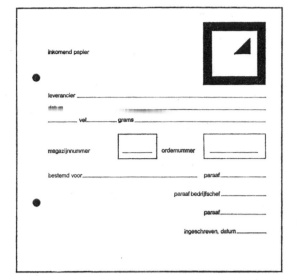

inkomend papier

leverancier _____

datum _____

_____ vel _____ grams _____

magazijnnummer [_____] ordernummer [_____]

bestemd voor _____ paraaf

paraaf bedrijfschef _____

paraaf _____

ingeschreven, datum _____

memo

aan: _____

datum: _____ uur: _____

onderwerp: _____

telefoonnummer: _____

_____

_____

_____

_____

_____

_____

_____

_____ van: _____

geen gehoor

onze bezorger kreeg héden bij u geen gehoor.

het (de) voor u bestemde pak(ken) hebben wij op het onderstaande adres afgegeven.

naam _____

adres _____

wilt u het (de) pak(ken) even af laten halen.

steendrukkerij de jong & co

zetwerk

zetterij/drukkerij _____

datum _____

werk _____ ordernummer [_____]

lettertype _____ soort _____ korps _____

zetbreedte _____ interlinie _____

vrije regelval blokvorm handzetsel machinezetsel proef op stroken proef opgemaakt

aantal proeven _____ aantal kunstdrukken _____ aantal barietdrukken _____

opdrachtgever namens steendrukkerij de jong & co; paraaf _____

postbus 86 - hilversum

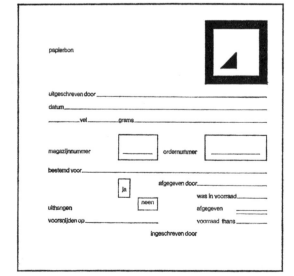

papierbon

uitgeschreven door _____

datum _____

_____ vel _____ grams _____

magazijnnummer [_____] ordernummer [_____]

bestemd voor _____

[ja] afgegeven door _____

was in voorraad _____

[neen] afgegeven _____

uithangen

voorsnijden op _____ voorraad thans _____

ingeschreven door

adreswijziging
change of address
changement d'adresse
adressen wechsel

wilt u de kwadraat-bladen aan mijn adres zenden
please send the quadrat-prints to my address
veuillez adresser les feuilles-cadrat à mon adresse
bitte richten sie die quadrat-blätter an meine anschrift

naam, name, nom, name: _____

straat, address, rue, strasse: _____

gemeente, city, lieu, ort: _____

provincie, state, province, kanton: _____

land, country, pays, land: _____

beroep, occupation, profession, beruf: _____

_____

_____

The Quadrat Prints published by Steendrukkerij de Jong & Co were part of a preconceived plan to build up the reputation of this small printing firm so that it could compete with larger companies. In these days of takeovers and mergers, a small company can only continue on its own by specialization. In the case of this printing plant, quality is its specialization. One of the results of publishing the Quadrat Prints has been a change in clientele. Designers have been attracted to the company because they have seen the high quality of the work produced and trust them to maintain it. For this standard they are willing to pay the higher prices which a small organization is obliged to charge. In the public's mind, art and quality are similar things, and by linking itself with an art publication Steendrukkerij de Jong & Co has strengthened its reputation for quality printing. A set of rules has been deliberately avoided by Steendrukkerij de Jong & Co for their publicity material which reaches the public, a high standard of production being the distinguishing feature. Within the company however, a rigid design policy has been adhered to. An example of this policy can be seen in the forms designed by Brattinga which are illustrated on the previous page. These incorporate a clock symbol in a square, each position of the hands of the clock representing a different stage in the production line of the printing firm. The handling of consignments is facilitated by these immediately recognizable symbols.

The Quadrat Prints were first published in 1955 and were the result of Brattinga's conviction that, in order to flourish, an industry must draw attention to itself. Any industry can advertise, but very few give anything in return, he believes. When the company concerned is a printing press it can send round ideas by other people, at the same time enhancing its own reputation by the quality of the printing. It could be a pinup or a reproduction of a painting, but Brattinga has always looked for the new and unusual. Articles on subjects which, though considered avantgarde, are comparatively accepted and known, will always be printed in other publications. Brattinga wants the Quadrat Prints to publish the very newest experimental work, the most original and advanced ideas which might otherwise never find an outlet.

The subject of each issue is decided by Brattinga. If he discovers someone working on a different and interesting idea, he encourages him to develop it, accompanying the development himself both in its content and from the technical side. The creation of the Print is, however, given over to an independent designer. There is no standard policy for the design of the Prints and within the basic form of the square the designer has a free hand. This gives a strongly individual flavour to each edition. There is no timetable or deadline for publication. The Prints are produced only when they have reached the highest possible standard, both in form and content. Although distributed in the main to clients, artists and designers throughout the world, the Prints can be obtained free on request while supplies are available.

The Quadrat Prints have received praise in the press all over the world:

All of these issues are not only fascinating in their contents but they also abound in graphic expression possible only to a printing company.

Katsumi, Masaki, 'Graphic Design', Tokyo, Japan; July 1962

In our own commercialized age cultural values tend to get trodden underfoot in the rush for quick profits, and the institutions that have made a point of upholding them deserve our unstinting recognition. One such company is Steendrukkerij de Jong & Co of Hilversum, that has never lost its respect for the artists as individuals and is today putting its own public relations policy at the service of good design and creative ideas. While personal contacts with artists have always been a tradition of the firm, the direct encouragement of creative art has been greatly intensified since 1952, when Pieter Brattinga took over the direction of this side of the firm's activities and launched such schemes as the now well-known Quadrat Prints and the exhibitions staged in the printing-house canteen.

Introduction to an article in 'Graphis' (number 115) by Walter Herdeg, Zürich, Switzerland September/October 1964

To Steendrukkerij de Jong & Co progress in the printing industry means more than increasing the speed of printing rollers.
The business principle that over the long run it pays to do a good job has found conclusive proof in the company's expansion.
In the printed matter published for the purpose of self-promotion we note an exemplary line. This printing-house takes its own medicine in that it practises what it recommends to others, namely the use of good material in advertising.
We are glad to see the Quadrat Prints here in Stuttgart, and will make them the subject of extensive discussion.

Anton Stankowski. Catalogue Landesgewerbe Amt, Stuttgart; 1966

'. . . . Its reputation has been remarkably magnified by occasional publication over several years, of Quadrat Prints. These are forthrightly avantgarde, written and designed by invitation, produced to the very highest intellectual and technical standards in limited editions of 2000, and sent as gifts to clients and friends all over the world . . . . Every public activity of this firm is a little masterpiece of taste, discreetly reinforcing its image at the highest level'.

'Design coordination and corporate image' by F. H. K. Henrion and Alan Parkin, Studio Vista, London, England; 1967

conway.

Chagall. Plea for mystery

For the clocks of Chagall, Pieter Brattinga took a litho stone to the South of France to persuade Chagall to make a lithograph on it *à l'instant*. The operation succeeded, the lithograph – actually a rather mediocre sample of Chagall's work – was included in the publication, accompanied by a text by Bernard Majorick. His contribution is an ideal example of what could be called a modern essay, (who contended that essayists had died out?), concise, clear and probing deeply, one would almost believe that one had come across a new Coleridge.

Majorick's article contains one of the most well-informed attacks on the Renaissance and post-Renaissance cultures, and at the same time one of the soundest pleas for 'an art of painting with mystery', I have ever read in any language. The fact that his appreciation of our modern media of culture is rather negative – and that he is rather inconsequent in his arguments – does not make any difference to the importance of his observations.

'Vrij Nederland', Amsterdam, Netherlands; January 1957

text: Bernard Majorick
litho: Marc Chagall
typography: Otto Treumann

Buckminster Fuller

This publication contains an extract from a letter by the famous American engineer in which he explains his working methods (translated into Dutch, French and German) and sketches and photographs of domes, of a beautiful graphic workmanship.

It should be mentioned that Buckminster Fuller's studies are no longer in the experimental stage, but have entered the field of industrialization. Consequently certain American firms at present manufacture certain types of his domes.

'L'Architecture d'Aujourd'hui', Paris, France; 1958
typography and design: Otto Treumann

Letters to the editor: Sandberg II

On a murky, rainy 30th of June 1959, people in the Netherlands once more took up the occupation of throwing dirty mops and smelly banana peels. The reason was Mr. Sandberg. Who else in the Netherlands can cause such an outburst of emotion? Mr. Sandberg has written a youthful post-script about which everybody, if he so wishes, can have his doubts.

When somebody thinks he has found this truth and puts it on paper, should he then be jumped upon, with the help of all the inquisition-boys one can find, and be put under lock and key accompanied by certain noises belonging to the Dark Ages, by loud shouting t.v. audiences. Should his nails be pulled out and should he be drawn and quartered and furthermore burnt at the stake of the newspaper district? That is what one does if one does not have a very strong opinion of one's own!

Amsterdam,   Opland

'Het Parool', Amsterdam, Netherlands; Saturday July 4th, 1959
text, typography and design: Sandberg

Les pendules de Chagall

The Clocks of Chagall

Chagall's Uhren

Ce que je vais vous dire à propos des pendules de Chagall n'a peut-être que peu à faire avec le peintre. Peut-être au contraire que tout cela a bien se rapporte à lui. Nous allons voir.

Le thème de la pendule revient dans l'œuvre de Chagall avec la régularité d'une pendule dont le balancier serait devenu quelque peu fantasque. Sur une toile (encore cubiste) de 1911, et dédiée à Apollinaire,

lignes vagues d'un cadran. En 1931, une pendule, cette fois bien distincte, avec une aile et une petite poupée à la place du balancier, constitue le motif central d'un paysage d'hiver. En 1933, la même pendule, de nouveau pourvue d'une aile, mais sans la petite poupée, revient dans une composition dédiée à la femme du peintre. Sur une toile de 1943, une pendule à la ligne flexible repose mollement, sur le bras d'un jongleur à tête d'oiseau. En 1946, plane une horloge à bras humaine au-dessus d'un portrait du peintre. En 1948, retour de l'horloge de 31 et de 33, avec cette différence que c'est un couple amoureux qui se tient à la place du balancier.

Parmi les thèmes en nombre tout de même limité auxquels a recours Chagall (un couple amoureux, le souvenir de Witebsk, l'homme au violon, l'homme et le violoncelle, le jongleur, le Christ, le soleil), c'est une place dominante que prend la pendule.

On peut croire avec certitude que Chagall lui-même aurait de la peine à nous fournir la plus petite explication concernant la symbolique de ses pendules. Pour ma part je suis d'ailleurs convaincu qu'on peut éprouver une satisfaction particulièrement vive à la vue de ses tableaux sans, par exemple, avoir été tout d'abord initié à certaines particularités folkloriques de la communauté judéo-russe qui y figurent assez souvent. Il faut être moins pour s'aimer un tableau qu'à partir du moment où l'on en connaît les sous-entendus iconographiques et symboliques. Des prétentions dans le sens pédagogique ou exégétique ont mais n'en a aucune. Il est écrit, avec les pendules comme point de départ, pour celui qui, aimant Chagall, se trouve parfois embarrassé vis-à-vis de ses relations d'affaires.

What I am going to say here in connection with the clocks of Chagall may have little to do with this painter. But perhaps it has very much to do with him. Let us see.

The theme of the clock recurs in Marc Chagall's work with the regularity of a somewhat wildly behaving pendulum. In a (still cubist) painting of 1911, dedicated to Apollinaire, Gendratt and Walden the first

clearly-to-be-distinguished wall-clock with a wing and a little doll at the place of the pendulum form the centre of a winter landscape. In 1933 the same clock returns, again with a wing, but now without a little doll, in a composition dedicated to the painter's wife. On a canvas of 1943 a clock hangs on the arm of a juggler with bird's head. In 1946 a clock with human hands hover over a self-portrait. In 1948: the return of the clock of 1931 and 1933 with this difference that now a love-couple lurks in the pendulum-case. Among the limited number of themes as it is that Chagall handles (love-couple, reminiscence of Witebsk, man with a violin, man with one's head, man with violoncelle, juggler, Christ, sun) the clock takes up a dominant place.

It may safely be assumed that Chagall himself will hardly be able to give us even the slightest explanation about the 'symbolism' of his clocks. I am however convinced of the fact that his pictures can afford one much pleasure, without — to mention something — having been informed beforehand of certain folk-loristic peculiarities of the Jewish-Russian community which pretty often appear on these canvases. Nobody, a mob excepted, ever began to like a painting at the moment that the iconographic and the symbolic implications were explained to him. This essay has no pretensions of a pedagogic or exegetic tendency. It was written, with the clocks as starting-point, for one, who bring a lover of Chagall's will with his love for this to-realise occasionally get into trouble with his business relations and who then hesitatingly crosses himself in the company of these heathens.

Was ich hier von Chagalls Uhren sage, hat vielleicht wenig mit diesem Maler zu tun. Möglicherweise aber auch sehr viel. Wir wollen einmal sehen.

Das Thema der Uhr kehrt in Marc Chagalls Werk mit der Regelmässigkeit eines steigernisens wildgewordenen Pendeluhrwerkes zurück. Auf einem (noch kubistischen Werk) aus dem Jahre 1911, das Apollinaire, Gendratt und Walden gewidmet ist, zeichnen

1931 bildet eine, nun deutlich erkennbare Wanduhr mit Flügel und einem Püppchen statt eines Pendels den Mittelpunkt einer Winterlandschaft. 1933 kehrt die gleiche Uhr wieder, gleichfalls mit einem Flügel, nun aber ohne Püppchen, auf einer, der Frau des Malers gewidmeten Komposition. Auf einem Bild aus dem Jahre 1943 hängt eine Uhr am Arm eines Jongleurs mit einem Vogelkopf. 1946 schwebt eine Uhr mit Menschenarmen über einem Selbstporträt. 1948: Wiederkehr der Uhr der Jahre 31 und '33 mit dem Unterschied, dass sich im Gehäuse ein Liebespaar befindet.

Unter der begrenzten Themenzahl Chagalls (Liebespaar, Erinnerung an Witebsk, Mann mit Enelskopf, Mann mit Geige, Gelist, Jongleur, Christus, Sohn) nimmt das Uhrwerk einen beherrschenden Raum ein. Man kann ruhig annehmen, dass Chagall selbst kaum imstande sein wird, uns Aufschluss über die Symbolik seiner Uhren zu geben. Ich bin aber davon überzeugt, dass man an seinen Malereien besonders viel Vergnügen erleben kann, ohne dass man — um nur etwas zu erwähnen — vorher über bestimmte folkloristische Eigentümlichkeiten der jüdisch-russischen Gemeinschaft unterrichtet ist, die auf den Bildern ab und zu vorkommen. Nur ein Snob erwärmt sich für ein Bild in dem Augenblick in dem ihm ikonographische oder symbolistische Hintergründigkeiten erklärt werden. Dieser Aufsatz ist also weder in pädagogischer noch in exegetischer Richtung prätentiös. Er ist für jemanden geschrieben, der Chagall schätzt und mit seiner Liebe zu dem It-Realisten seinen Geschäftsfreunden gegenüber in Verlegenheit kommt und dann in Gesellschaft dieser Heiden zögert, ein

Buckminster Fuller

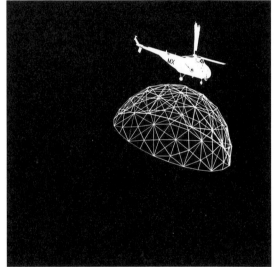

14

Now the machine, Ton de Leeuw on 'Music and Technics'

In 'Music and Engineering' Ton de Leeuw makes an interesting comparison in words and pictures between primitive music from time immemorial and the electronic sounds of today. Starting with the simple use of wood, metal, stretched animal skins and strings on which man drummed and strummed, the range of instruments developed to the flute, overgrown with valves, and the piano, just as complicated in construction as the modern composing machine . . .

'Haagse Post', Amsterdam, Netherlands; April 2nd, 1960

text: Ton de Leeuw
typographic design: Harry Sierman

Written Language

'Written Language' is an anthology of modern poetry collected by Simon Vinkenoog. Poets and their handwriting . . . . handwriting which at a first glance does not seem to differ from the handwriting of commercial travellers, handwritings of members of the House of Lords, handwriting of beauty-queens.
But behind this handwriting, in these poets' handwriting, the poem is hidden, the modern poem with its own forms and contents, a cross-section of the world in 1961. This collection will be extended in the future, and will constitute a living collection of poetry, written language, food for graphologists.

'Radio-Televisie week', Brussels, Belgium; March 4th, 1961

editor: Simon Vinkenoog
typography: Ton Raateland

Bruno Munari and his 'Unreadable Books', Tokachiyo Uemura

Bruno Munari's 'unreadable books' are striking rather than original. To readers, books that can't be read should be striking, and to painters, picturebooks that entirely lack pictures should be striking too. Likewise publications without lettering or design must be striking to designers.
This is such a book. Not one letter is printed anywhere in it. The book is just sheets of good quality red and white paper bound together. Each page has different shapes, both horizontal and vertical, cut out of it. Therefore, by various combinations of turned pages many geometrical, abstract pictures in red and white, like Mondrian's, will be produced. Not only can the combinations be made entirely of one's own free will, but there is an immense number of variations, and so one can have the pleasure of producing as many abstract pictures as desired. In use it becomes a more interesting book-toy than picture books which are simply for 'reading' or 'seeing', and this prevents boredom from setting in. So this is really a strange book . . .

'Idea', Tokyo, Japan; 1963
creator: Bruno Munari

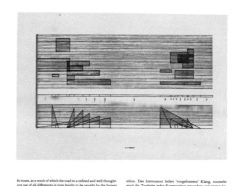

80 tones, as a result of which the road to a refined and well thought-out use of all differences in tone height ought to be caught by the human ear is cut off. But this is going to change, too. The great achievement of technical control of sound inevitably leads us to changed concepts and possibilities in almost every field. But all this will no doubt only be completely realized in the future. And the musical control of all this has hardly come beyond the phase of wishful thinking...

But where do we make a start? Only a few centuries have passed since Europe saw signs of the rise of independent instrumental music. The first expressions of this music still leaned heavily on the forms of vocal music that had known its heydays in a previous period. Yet, they have given us the greatest instrumental creations:

sition. Das Instrument liefert 'vorgeformten' Klang, oftmals wird die Tonfarbe jeder Komposition gesondert und erneut bestimmt. Aber dies darf man auch bei den anderen Tonelementen erwarten. So geht die klassische Musik von einer verhältnismässig groben und fixierten Tonreihe von etwa achtzig Tönen aus, der gleichschwebenden Temperatur. Der Weg zu einer verfeinerten und verantwortungsvollen Verwendung aller von uns wahrnehmbaren Höhenunterschiede wurde somit versperrt. Auch dies wird sich ändern. Die Beherrschung des Schalles führt uns zwangsläufig zu veränderten Konzeptionen und Möglichkeiten auf fast jedem Gebiete. Vieles wird sich aber zweifellos erst in Zukunft vollständig verwirklichen lassen. Und die musikalische Beherrschung ist noch kaum aus dem Stadium des Wunschtraumes herausgekommen.

18

Organics

The issue of 'Organics' under review was designed by the editor of the series, Professor Pieter Brattinga himself, while its author is designer William Katavolos, born in New York of Greek parentage in 1924. The very attractive publication deals with his ideas about chemical architecture. It is no longer to be built, but should grow organically out of chemically produced, powdered and liquid materials which, when treated with certain activating agents, expand enormously, then catalyze and harden. Thus the new city on the sea is formed out of large circles of an oily substance into which a plastic mass is poured; it forms a network of strips and discs that expand into swellings and shells, then, perforated, form cavities. Double walls containing chemicals replace the windows, and the fixed floors provide all the necessities for living. The chair of synthetic resin, blown double-walled, filled with chemicals, not only rises and descends, but also vibrates, cools, heats and even contains electronic devices for sound and for creating ionic fields. Containers, created according to the same system, can cool, cook, and replace stoves, sinks and store rooms. In the double-walled container the occupant not only takes a chemical vapour bath, but is also washed and dried. Employed as a lavatory, the container rises and lowers as required and also dissolves the waste products chemically in such a way that sewage pipes become superfluous. In cities composed of such houses the suburbs can unite in the morning into one city, and at night can move to other places.
All that sounds like a scurrilous dream, particularly when looking at the fantastically pertinent drawings, but who will assert that it will not materialize tomorrow?

'Möbel und Dekoration', Stuttgart, Germany; October 1962

text: William Katavolos
typography and design: Pieter Brattinga

Op de grondslagen der scheikunde kan een nieuwe architectuur worden opgebouwd. De mens zou moeten ophouden met maken en manipuleren, en in plaats daarvan de architectuur zelf haar gang moeten laten gaan. Er zijn mogelijkheden die verder gaan dan bouwen, zoals het beginsel van golven, parabolische banen en loodlijnen ook bestaat zonder de stoffelijke lichamen die er aan gehoorzamen. Op dezelfde wijze moet de architectuur zich vrijmaken van de traditionele vormenleer en organisch worden.

Nieuwe ontdekkingen van de chemie hebben geleid tot de produktie van poedervormige en vloeibare stoffen die, wanneer ze worden behandeld met bepaalde activerende agentia, zich sterk uitzetten om verwijgene te katalyseren en een vaste vorm aan te nemen. Onze kennis omtrent de moleculaire structuur van deze stoffen naamt snel toe, tezamen met de nodige technieken voor de produktie van materialen die, zich nog in het submicroscopische stadium bevinden, van een "ingebouwd" gedragspatroon worden voorzien. Evenzo zal het mogelijk worden minieme hoeveelheden poeder te namen en deze te doen uitzetten tot van te voren bepaalde vormen zoals bollen, buizen en ringen.

A new architecture is possible through the matrix of chemistry. Man must stop making and manipulating, and instead slow architecture to happen. There is a way beyond building just as the principles of waves, parabolas and plummet lines exist beyond the mediums in which they form. So must architecture free itself from traditional patterns and become organic.

New discoveries in chemistry have led to the production of powdered and liquid materials which when suitably treated with certain activating agents expand to great size and then catalize and become rigid. We are rapidly gaining the necessary knowledge of the molecular structure of these chemicals, together with the necessary techniques that will lead to the production of materials which will have a specific program of behavior built into them, while still in the sub-microscopic stage. Accordingly it will be possible to take minute quantities of powder and make them expand into pre-determined shapes such as spheres, tubes and toruses.

La naissance d'une architecture nouvelle est possible grâce à la chimie. Il faut que l'homme, abandonnant ses travaux et ses manipulations, laisse l'architecture naître spontanément. Derrière l'activité du constructeur, il y a une force indépendante, comme derrière les ondes, les trajectoires paraboliques et le fil à plomb, il y a des principes existant indépendamment des instruments par lesquels ils se manifestent. L'architecture doit ainsi se libérer des formes conventionnelles et devenir fonctionnelle.

En chimie, de nouvelles découvertes ont permis la production, sous forme de poudres ou de liquides, de substances qui, lorsqu'elles subissent l'action de certains agents activents, acquièrent en se dilatant un grand volume, puis se solidifient par catalyse. La science progresse rapidement vers une connaissance de la structure moléculaire de ces agents chimiques; en même temps, nous sommes en train de maîtriser des techniques qui permettront de produire des matériaux dont le comportement futur sera réglé alors qu'ils seront encore à l'état sub-microscopique. De la sorte, on pourra obtenir, par dilation, des objets de forme prédéterminée (sphères, tubes, tores . . .)

Die Chemie eröffnet uns neue Wege in der Architektur. Man soll nicht mehr mühsam konstruieren, sondern die Architektur als Geschehnis ermöglichen. Es gibt einen Weg ausserhalb des Bauens, gerade so wie das Prinzip der Wellen, Parabelwürfe und Lotlinien ausserhalb des Mediums liegt, in welchem sie sich bilden. So muss sich die Architektur von althergebrachter Vorbildern lösen und organisch werden.

Dank neuen Erfindungen in der Chemie können pulverförmige und flüssige Stoffe hergestellt werden, die sich durch entsprechende Behandlung mit bestimmten aktivierenden Agentien gewaltig ausdehnen, dann katalysieren und erhärten. Wir gewinnen immer mehr Kenntnisse der Molekularstruktur dieser Chemikalien sowie der nötigen Verfahren zur Herstellung von Stoffen mit einem bereits im submikroskopischen Stadium bestimmbaren Verhalten. Es wird also möglich sein, sehr kleine Mengen Pulver so zu verarbeiten, dass sie sich zu vorbestimmten Formen wie Schalen, Röhren und Wulsten ausdehnen.

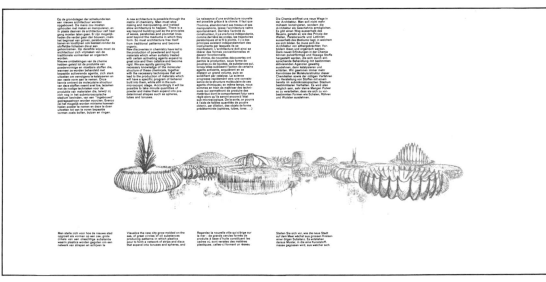

Men stelle zich voor hoe de nieuwe stad opgroeit als vormen op een zee, grote cirkels van een olieachtige substantie waarin plastics worden gegoten om een netwerk van strepen en schijven te

Visualize the new city grow molded on the sea, of great circles of oil substances producing patterns in which plastics that expand into toruses and spheres, and

Regardez la nouvelle ville qui s'érige sur la mer : de grands cercles formés de poudres ou de liquides, de substances qui, à base d'huile constituent les cadres où, sont versées des matières plastiques; celles-ci forment un réseau

Stellen Sie sich vor, wie die neue Stadt auf dem Meer wächst aus grossen Kreisen einer öligen Substanz. Es entstehen daraus Muster, in die eine Kunststoffmasse gegossen wird, aus welcher sich

---

Een dergelijk huis zou kunnen uitdijen tot een bepaalde grootte, zich onderverdelen of samensmelten met andere. Men zou grote gewelven kunnen vormen door parabolische straalsgewijs vormen wanneer ze met de lucht in contact komen. Uitdijende lichamen, onmiddellijk ontstaande uit een explosiegewijze transformaties, in alle gewenste dichtheden, in bekende richtingen en gedurende voorfbereikende tijdsduren.

Houses such as this would grow to certain sizes, sub-divide or fuse for larger functions. Great vaults could be produced with parabolic jets that catalize on contact with the air. Exploding patterns of an instanteneous architecture of transformations, into desired densities, into known directions, for calculated durations.

De telles demeures pourraient atteindre certaines dimensions, se subdiviser, ou se grouper en unités aux fonctions plus étendues. On lancerait de hautes voûtes par projections paraboliques qui durciraient au contact de l'air. Structures explosives, fruits d'une architecture instantanée de transformation, ayant des densités précises, des directions connues,

Solche Häuser würden zu einer bestimmten Grösse anwachsen, sich unterteilen oder zu grossen Komplexen verschmelzen. Riesige Gewölbe würden durch Parabelwürfe aus Kunstharz hergestellt, die in Verbindung mit der Luft katalysieren. Explosionsartig entstehende Formen einer unmittelbaren Architektur, Verwandlungen in gewünschte Festigkeiten, in bekannte Richtungen und für

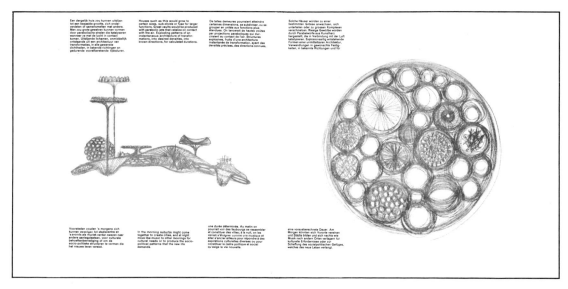

Voorstaleden zouden 's morgens zich kunnen verenigen tot stadscentra en 's avonds als muziek verder rezien naar andere aanlegplaatsen, voor culturele behoeftenbevrediging of om de socio-politieke structuren te vormen die het nieuwe leven verlangt.

In the morning suburbs might come together to create cities, and at night move like music to different moorings for cultural needs or to produce the socio-political patterns that the new life demands.

une durée déterminée. Au matin on pourrait voir des faubourgs se rassembler et constituer des villes; à la nuit, on les verrait s'éloigner comme une musique et aller s'ancrer ailleurs pour répondre à des aspirations culturelles diverses ou pour constituer le cadre politique et social que exige la vie nouvelle.

eine vorausberechnete Dauer. Am Morgen könnten sich Vororte vereinen und Städte bilden und sich nachts wie Musik nach andern Orten verlagern für kulturelle Erfordernisse oder zur Schaffung des soziopolitischen Gefüges, welches das neue Leben verlangt.

Rietveld 1924, Schröderhuis

Rietveld's best known work is a building of modest dimensions that, though not yet forty years old, should already be considered a classic. It is the house Rietveld built in 1924 for Mrs. T. Schröder in the Prins Hendriklaan in Utrecht. In no other building have the intentions of 'de Stijl' been more purely realized, and this house, not built without opposition, is at present the goal of many an architectural pilgrimage.
It is of great importance that extensive documentation on this building is now available. This Quadrat Print contains the original 1924 drawings of the three outside walls, the plans, the perspective sketches, and new colour photographs of the building. In addition there are recent comments by the architect, reproduced in his handwriting. Thanks to this completeness this Quadrat Print is a valuable document for all those who are interested in modern architecture and design.
The simple, constructive typographic forms harmonize excellently with the subject. The designer-editor has managed to combine the heterogeneous elements: drawings, colour photographs, handwriting and translations (composed from founder's type), in a well-ordered manner. Its subject matter, design and execution make this publication one of value, in more than one respect.

'Intergrafia', Amsterdam, Netherlands; June 10th, 1963

architectural drawings (1924) and text: Rietveld
photographs (1963) and design: Pieter Brattinga

Rietveld, 1924.
Schröder Huis

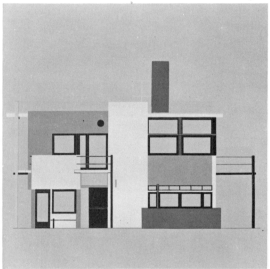

Ook aan deze zijkant is het vlak met gaten
vervangen door de tegenstellingen: dicht open
met enige vlakken in de drie verschillende
richtingen
De kleuren grijs en wit versterken de openheid;
hier is geprobeerd de grensvlakken van het interieur
naar buiten duidelijk te tonen.

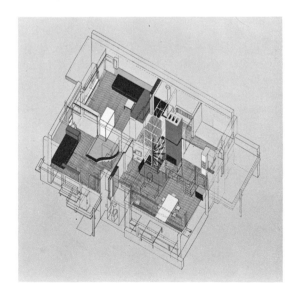

Deze scherpe projectie geeft een (misschien wat
schemerige) indruk van de poging om binnen en buiten
tot een ruimtebeeld te verwerken.
De buitenwanden zijn gesplitst in open en dichte
gedeelten; het doorgaand vlak met gaten'' is vermeden.
Om tot een visueel samenspel te komen van
wanden en vloer, zijn de verschillende eisen, die het
gebruik aan de vloerbedekking stelde, gebruikt om een
verdeling in kleur, materiaal, licht en donker te maken.

Written Language II

For the second edition of these Quadrat-Prints 'Schrijf-taal' (Written Language) which appeared for the first time in 1961, Simon Vinkenoog has selected modern poems. Even the colour contrasts of the paper are remarkable: olive-green, blue-green, blue and orange, blue-grey, pink, beige and white. Each of the 19 poets was allocated 4 pages, only one of which contains a poem which is reproduced in the poet's handwriting, while the fourth contains a few points such as name, birthplace, date of birth, booktitles etc. Eight of the poets write in Dutch, three in English, four in French, one in German and three in Russian. With one exception, all of them give even the layman some insight into their character by means of the lively handwriting together with their poem.

'Möbel und Dekoration,' Stuttgart, Germany; April 1964

editor: Simon Vinkenoog
typography: Ton Raateland

Genesis of a Composition

... 'Genesis of a Composition' written by Bernard Majorick, refers to a wall painting made by Jan Bons in 1952 on the straw wall of the Netherlands pavilion in Mexico. In this four-language manuscript, with a reproduction of the design, the author tries to recapture the origin of the painting from the available sketches. Art philosophy and suppositions suggest he had access to Bons' 'kitchen'. This concise study is interestingly written, and evokes appreciation and admiration for Bons, who probably has never had his work explained so clearly before.

'Het Parool', Amsterdam, Netherlands; December 23rd, 1961

text: Bernard Majorick
typography and design: Jan Bons

Non-Games, Jasia Reichardt

... The book consists of 60 loose-leaf pages, each of which is a blow-up of a small section of the English Daily Mirror. Diter Rot himself wrote about it as follows: 'they are part of a group of books I made in the year 1962 out of a bunch of Daily Mirrors –' ... instead of showing quality (surprising quality), we show quantity (surprising quantity). I got this idea (Quantity instead of Quality) in this way: 'Quality' is business (for example advertising), is just a subtle way of being Quantity-minded: Quality in advertising wants expansion and (in the end) power=quantity. So, let us produce Quantities for once!' ...

'Studio', London, England; March 1968
creator: Diter Rot

Schrijf—taal ii·

WRITTEN LANGUAGE / LANGUE ÉCRITE / GESCHRIEBENE SPRACHE

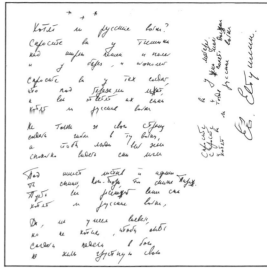

GENESIS
VAN
EEN
COMPOSITIE

En 1952 se tint l'exposition "Asi es Holanda". Elle fut organisée par l'architecte G. Rietveld, qui conseilla de faire faire par le peintre Jan Bons une peinture murale sur la façade extérieure de l'exposition. Cette peinture murale de 77 m de long sur 6 m de haut fut peinte à la peinture émulsive sur des nattes de jonc. La commande de cette peinture murale fut donnée par le service d'Information du Gouvernement Néerlandais et fut réalisée grâce à l'aide de la Fondation Prince Bernard.

1952 wurde in Mexiko City die Ausstellung "Asi es Holanda" veranstaltet. Sie wurde vom Architekten G. Rietveld eingerichtet, der empfahl, den Künstler Jan Bons mit der Anfertigung einer Wandmalerei an der Aussenfront der Ausstellung zu betrauen. Diese Wandmalerei, die 77 M. lang und 6 M. hoch war, wurde mit Emulsionfarbe auf Rohrmatten gemalt. Der Auftrag für diese Wandmalerei wurde vom Niederländischen Regierungs-Aufklärungsamt erteilt und kam mit Hilfe des "Prins Bernhard-Fonds" zustande.

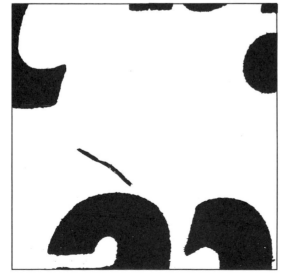

Pim & Philomene

Pim van Boxsel had just made his first drawing for the Dutch weekly, 'De Nieuwe Linie', in March 1966, when he was commissioned by Brattinga to compose a comic-strip story in four languages for the 'Quadrat Prints' series. Hence, the only words occurring in the seventy three pages of drawings are 'olé, hop, ah, oh and rrraaaggg'. 'How is it possible to effect communication without text, just by means of photos and drawings?' Said Brattinga, 'My request to Pim van Boxsel was to tell a story in drawings. I am curious to know what the outcome will be'... What came out is the most communicative thing in existence, namely the story of a certain Philomene, who allows herself to be led amorously from picture to picture by intercontinental destiny: space-travellers, maharajas and decamerone-Italians compete for her favours, which she does not grant completely unwillingly.

'De Nieuwe Linie', Amsterdam, Netherlands; March 11th, 1967

script and illustrations: Pim van Boxsel
design: Pieter Brattinga

New Alphabet
Alphabet of Poverty
... What it is about

Crouwel's undertaking is indicated as a 'Proposal for a new typeface that is more suitable than traditional type for the composing system by means of a cathode-ray tube.
... There is something not right there. The faces, designed one by one with great care, need similar attention in composing. The faces are designed by intuition and the human shortcomings in them often constituted their charm and character, but this also implied that optical correction in composing was essential. Such a task, of course, can only be partially taken over by a machine, and only partially too even when the most elaborate computer is employed. The precision of the human eye coupled with feeling can never be replaced by a machine ... That is where something is not right.

'Intergrafia', Amsterdam, Netherlands; November 20th, 1967
text and design: Wim Crouwel

Henry Miller

This latest edition, which as an exception could sooner be termed curious than experimental, consists of three water-colours specially brushed for the Quadrat Prints by the nestor of literary sex-candour, Henry Miller, a few weeks before he married the young and beautiful Japanese singer Hoki Tokuda. That inspired him to water-colour ebullitions such as Hoki-doki, Happy days are here again, All the world loves a lover. Although a certain doubt seems to creep in on another sheet in cries such as Elle ne m'aime pas! Pourquoi? Soyons heureux quand-même! La vie n'est pas si dure, Zut alors! A nude of her might raise some doubts as to his potency, that is as a pictorial artist. But on the last sheet it is again the child that speaks – little woman, little cottage, little tree, little animal – the child that this invincible man, who wishes to be in love until his death, has possibly always been. Hoki-doki!

'Algemeen Handelsblad', Amsterdam, Netherlands; November, 30th, 1967

illustrations: Henry Miller
design cover: Pieter Brattinga

42

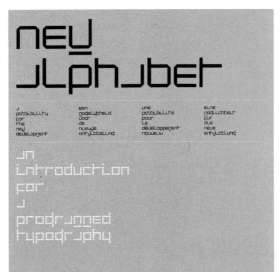

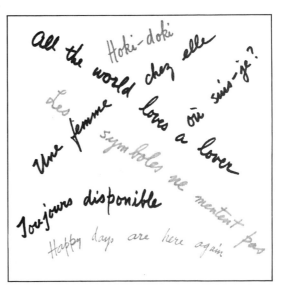

NU 2, Lambert Tegenbosch

In the summer of 1959 a rather innocuous article by W. Sandberg, then director of the Amsterdam Stedelijk Museum, started off an enormous uproar. The article appeared in a Quadrat Print entitled Nu, a public relations gift of Steendrukkerij de Jong in Hilversum, which apart from its attractive typographical design had nothing very memorable to offer.
Insignificant though the text was in itself, it naturally acquired moment through the simple circumstance that it had been written by none other than the director of the Amsterdam Stedelijk Museum. Since then nine years have gone by. Sandberg has moved from Amsterdam to Jerusalem, but he remains actively involved in the problems of today's welfare states as is evidenced by Nu 2, now on its way to Steendrukkerij de Jong's relations.
His words are unlikely to raise much of a stir. They do not open up new vistas, do not offer new insights and are hardly fit to provoke anyone. This time they derive their interest from the influence Sandberg had here for a range of decades.

'De Volkskrant', Amsterdam, Netherlands; October 23rd 1968
text and design: Willem Sandberg

 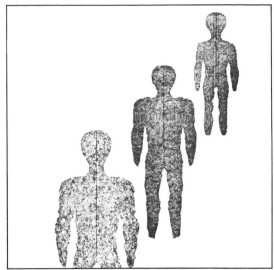

Posters

Posters announcing exhibitions at Steendrukkerij de Jong & Co are designed by Pieter Brattinga and are always of the same dimensions. He has made the square the symbol of the company's cultural activities and the posters are designed using a grid system of squares.
This grid system, sometimes apparent, often forming an unseen pattern, coordinates the posters giving them an easily recognizable identity. Occasionally the squares are introduced pictorially, making a visual joke of the symbol, an example being the poster for the exhibition of Topor's work.
The posters are never produced from finished sketches but are compiled by Steendrukkerij de Jong & Co from detailed instructions sent to them by Brattinga. This method is greatly facilitated by the use of a grid system, as explicit directions can be easily given for the placing of words and pictorial material.

Meanwhile, such younger designers in the Netherlands as Wim Crouwel and Pieter Brattinga were discovering the delights of greatly enlarged letter forms, which showed the irregularities of cutting and impression in imprecise edges, as a means of modifying the purity of their designs and imposing a sense of vibrancy and handwork on their book covers and posters (page 110).

World and Image/Posters from the Collection of The Museum of Modern Art/Selected and edited by Mildred Constantine/Text by Alan M. Fern; publ. The Museum of Modern Art, New York, New York, 1969.

Grid system for posters

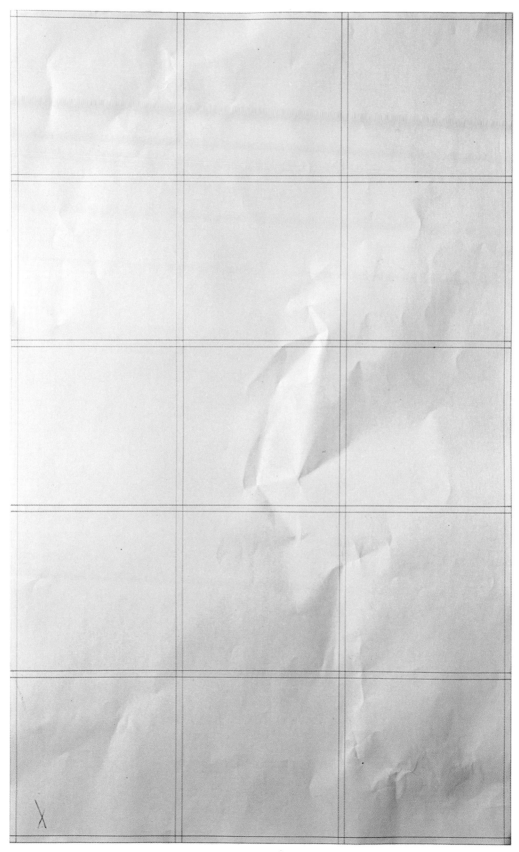

49

Man in Moscow, 1961, see also page 131

Poster for an exhibition of photographs of the Soviet citizen in his capital.

design: Pieter Brattinga

man in moskou
человек в москве

15 juli tot 15 september

tien uur tot half twaalf en twee tot vijf uur

zaterdags tien uur tot half twaalf

zondags gesloten

tentoonstelling

foto's van eddy posthuma de boer

фото: эдди постхума де бур

kantine

steendrukkerij de Jong & Co

's-gravelandseweg 19 bij de kei hilversum

Architectural Review, 1961, see also page 141

Poster for display of the typography of the magazine Architectural Review 1961, An exhibition of pages and designs from this British architectural magazine.

design: Pieter Brattinga

de typografie van het tijdschrift architectural review

Strijbosch '59, 1960

Poster for an exhibition of paintings by Wim Strijbosch, the recently deceased Dutch painter.

design: Pieter Brattinga

stuijbosch '59

tentoonstelling

van 28 november tot 31 december

tien uur tot half twaalf en twee tot vijf uur

zaterdags tien uur tot half twaalf

zondags gesloten

kantine

steendrukkerij de Jong & Co

's-gravelandseweg 19 bij de kei hilversum

55

A phase in vases 1895-1925, 1966, see also page 119

Poster announcing an exhibition of vases of the Art Nouveau period collected by Pieter Groot from the Amsterdam Flea Market.

design: Pieter Brattinga

56

een fase in vazen 1895-1925

11 december 1965 tot 11 februari 1966
10.00-11.30/14.00-17.00 uur
zaterdags en zondags gesloten

tentoonstelling

kantine
steendrukkerij de Jong & Co
printers, imprimeurs, drucker / offset-lithographic
's-gravelandseweg 19, hilversum, holland

Manhole covers in the Streets of New York, 1964, see also page 135

Poster for an exhibition of rubbings of manhole covers from the streets of New York.

design: Pieter Brattinga

58

putdeksels in de straten van new york

22 augustus tot 18 september 1964
10.00-11.30/14.00-17.00 uur
zaterdags en zondags gesloten

tentoonstelling

kantine
steendrukkerij de Jong & Co
printers, imprimeurs, drucker / offset- lithographic
's-gravelandseweg 19, hilversum, holland

59

The typography of Sandberg, 1958, see also page 117

Poster for an exhibition of the typographic designs of Wil Sandberg. Catalogues, posters, the series Experimenta Typographica (in manuscript and print) and various other typographic materials.

designs: Pieter Brattinga

tentoonstelling

van 19 mei tot 30 juni

tien uur tot half twaalf en twee tot vijf uur

zaterdags tien uur tot half twaalf

zondags gesloten

de typografie

van sandberg

kantine

steendrukkerij de Jong & Co

's-gravelandseweg 19 bij de kei hilversum

Dear James Bond, 1965

Poster for an exhibition of award-winning children's drawings from a competition about James Bond.

design: Pieter Brattinga

tekeningen: lieve james bond

20 oktober tot 30 oktober 1965
10.00-11.30/14.00-17.00 uur
zaterdags en zondags gesloten

tentoonstelling

kantine
steendrukkerij de Jong & Co
printers, imprimeurs, drucker / offset-lithographic
's-gravelandseweg 19, hilversum, holland

Graphic designs for a Canadian Railway Company, 1963, see also page 147

Poster for display of designs giving the corporate image of the Canadian National Railways.

design: Pieter Brattinga

grafische ontwerpen voor een canadese spoorwegmaatschappij

tentoonstelling

16 februari tot 10 april 1963

tien uur tot half twaalf en twee tot vijf uur

zaterdags gesloten

zondags gesloten

kantine

steendrukkerij de Jong & Co

's-gravelandseweg 19 bij de kei hilversum

Designs by Ikko Tanaka, 1965

Poster for an exhibition of designs by the Japanese graphic designer Ikko Tanaka.

design: Pieter Brattinga

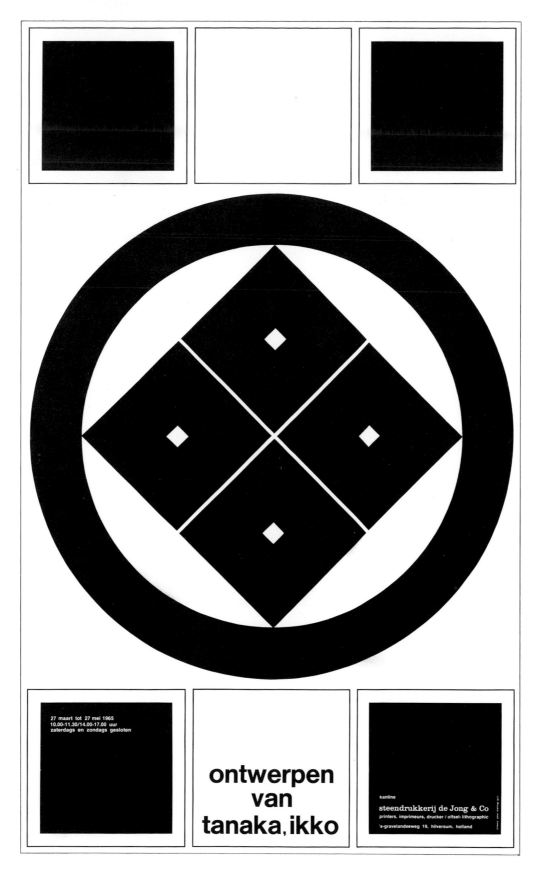

27 maart tot 27 mei 1965
10.00-11.30/14.00-17.00 uur
zaterdags en zondags gesloten

ontwerpen
van
tanaka, ikko

kantine
steendrukkerij de Jong & Co
printers, imprimeurs, drucker / offset-lithographic
's-gravelandseweg 19, hilversum, holland

On show are 500 covers by Dick, 1962, see also page 129

Poster for an exhibition of 500 covers designed by Dick Bruna on the occasion of the publication of the 500th paperback in the series 'Zwarte Beertjes'.

design: Pieter Brattinga.

Prints of wood-type from the collection of Kelly, 1965, see also page 125

Poster for an exhibition of prints from Rob Roy Kelly's collection of wood-type.

design: Pieter Brattinga

afdrukken van houten letters uit de verzameling van kelly

23 januari tot 4 maart 1965
10.00-11.30/14.00-17.00 uur
zaterdags en zondags gesloten

tentoonstelling

kantine
steendrukkerij de Jong & Co
printers, imprimeurs, drucker / offset- lithographic
's-gravelandseweg 19, hilversum, holland

Form and aerial photograph, 1960, see also page 135

Poster for a display of photographs from the topographical services. The photographs show various patterns which were compared with reproductions of paintings to show similarities in basic forms.

design: Pieter Brattinga

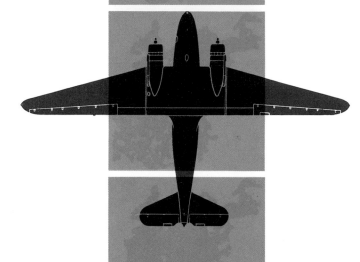

tentoonstelling

vorm en luchtfoto

van 9 juni tot 5 juli

tien uur tot half twaalf en twee tot vijf uur

zaterdags tien uur tot half twaalf

zondags gesloten

kantine

steendrukkerij de Jong & Co

s-gravelandseweg 19 bij de kei hilversum

Drawings by Opland, 1959, see also page 121

Poster for an exhibition of political drawings by Opland. Besides the drawings which Opland makes for Dutch newspapers, the Groene and the Volkskrant, details of his studio and home were reproduced in actual size in the exhibition hall together with some of his other drawings and paintings.

design: Pieter Brattinga

tentoonstelling

tekeningen van opland

kantine

steendrukkerij de Jong & Co

's-gravelandseweg 19 bij de kei hilversum

van 12 september tot 15 oktober

tien uur tot half twaalf en twee tot vijf uur

zaterdags tien uur tot half twaalf

zondags gesloten

75

Artificial food, 1960, see also page 133

On the occasion of the 40th exhibition the public was offered an 'art'ificial dinner in the form of material which is exhibited in shopwindows and plaster replicas of items of food, made by the baker's school in Amsterdam.
This can be regarded as one of the first pop-art exhibitions in the Netherlands (see catalogue 'Nieuw Realisme' 1964, Gemeente Museum 's-Gravenhage).

design: Pieter Brattinga

kunsteten

27 februari tot 16 maart

tien uur tot half twaalf en twee tot vijf uur

zaterdags tien uur tot half twaalf

zondags gesloten

kantine

steendrukkerij de Jong & Co

's-gravelandseweg 19 bij de kei hilversum

Lubalin's typography for the Saturday Evening Post, 1962

Poster announcing an exhibition of Lubalin's designs for the Saturday Evening Post. Some typical pages and double spreads were shown.

design: Pieter Brattinga

tentoonstelling

22 september tot 25 oktober 1962

tien uur tot half twaalf en twee tot vijf uur

zaterdags gesloten

zondags gesloten

lubalin's typografie voor de saturday evening post

kantine

steendrukkerij de Jong & Co

's-gravelandseweg 19 bij de kei hilversum

Architecture of L. Mies van der Rohe, 1959

Poster for an exhibition showing photographs and designs by the architect Mies v.d. Rohe. A sound tape with van der Rohe's voice talking about his philosophy completed this exhibition.

design: Pieter Brattinga

tentoonstelling

architektuur I. mies van der rohe

7 februari tot 14 maart

tien uur tot half twaalf en twee tot vijf uur

zaterdags tien uur tot half twaalf

zondags gesloten

kantine

steendrukkerij de Jong & Co

's-gravelandseweg 19 bij de kei hilversum

aanbouw greenwald-flatgebouw chicago

Topor Panique, 1966

Poster for a display of cartoons by the French artist Topor. The exhibition was on show in cubicles which were hung from the ceiling.

design: Pieter Brattinga drawing: Topor

11 juni tot 30 augustus 1966
10.00-11.30/14.00-17.00 uur
zaterdags en zondags gesloten

kantine
steendrukkerij de Jong & Co
printers, imprimeurs, drucker / offset-lithographic
's-gravelandseweg 19, hilversum, holland

topor: paniek

TOPOR

Quadrat Art by Karl Gerstner 1964, see also page 127

Poster for an exhibition of square paintings by the Swiss artist Karl Gerstner.

design: Pieter Brattinga

84

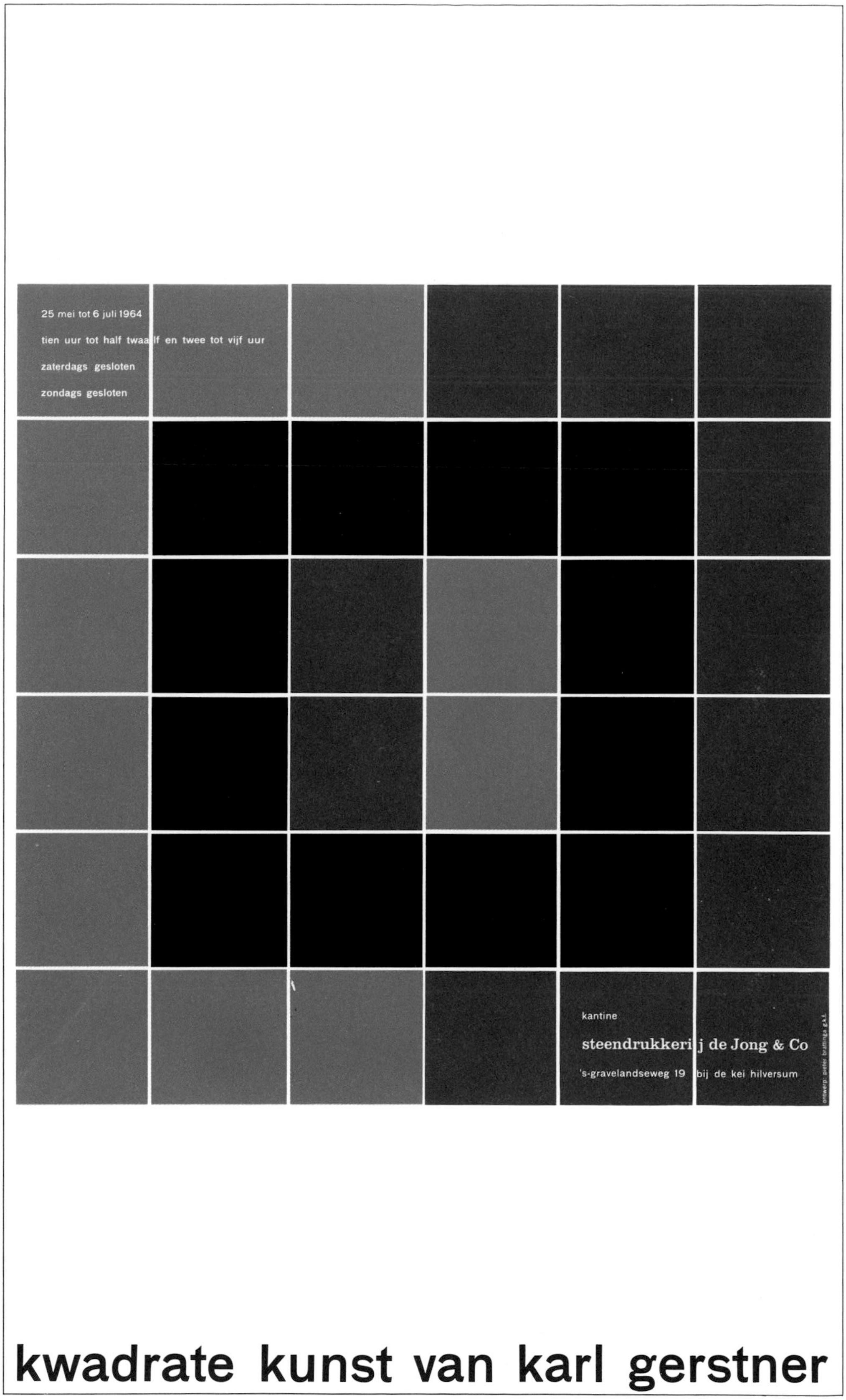

25 mei tot 6 juli 1964

tien uur tot half twaalf en twee tot vijf uur

zaterdags gesloten

zondags gesloten

kantine

steendrukkerij de Jong & Co

's-gravelandseweg 19 bij de kei hilversum

ontwerp: pieter brattinga g.k.f.

kwadrate kunst van karl gerstner

The man behind the design of the post office, 1960

Poster for an exhibition of architecture, industrial design, graphic design and interior design under the direction of the esthetic consultant to the Netherlands Post Office, Chris de Moor. The exhibition was supplemented with the personal paintings and drawings of Mr. de Moor.

design: Pieter Brattinga

de man achter de vormgeving van de p.t.t.

...ember tot 12 oktober
...half twaalf en twee tot vijf
...tot half twaalf

tentoonstelling

...steendrukkerij de Jong &
...g bij de ka. bken
chris de moor

Graphic design: Columbia Broadcasting System + Hessischer Rundfunk, 1959, see also page 129

Poster for an exhibition of graphic design for an American and a German broadcasting corporation. This exhibition shows different approaches in two different countries to a similar problem.

design: Pieter Brattinga

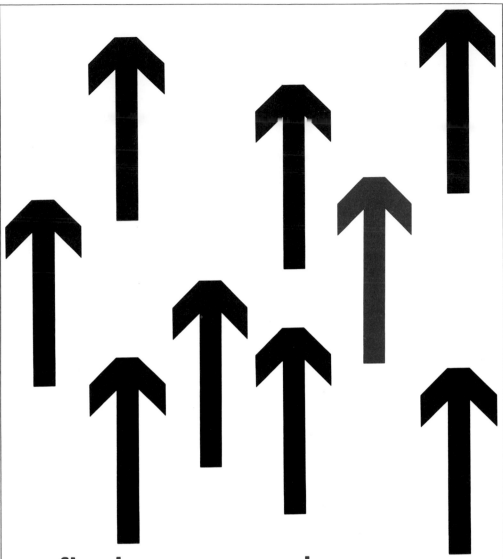

grafische vormgeving
columbia broadcasting system
hessischer rundfunk

tentoonstelling

30 mei tot 25 juni

tien uur tot half twaalf en twee tot vijf uur

zaterdags tien uur tot half twaalf

zondags gesloten

kantine

steendrukkerij de Jong & Co

's-gravelandseweg 19 bij de kei hilversum

Van Golden, 1966, see also page 153

Poster announcing an exhibition of comparatively new work by the Dutch painter van Golden. Works created in 1965 were on show.

design: Pieter Brattinga

conway·

2 september tot 28 oktober 1966
10.00-11.30/14.00-17.00 uur
zaterdags en zondags gesloten

tentoonstelling

kantine
steendrukkerij de Jong & Co
printers, imprimeurs, drucker / offset-lithographic
's-gravelandseweg 19, hilversum, holland

van golden negentien vijf en zestig

Japanese toys, 1962, see also page 135

An exhibition of Japanese children's toys.

design: Pieter Brattinga

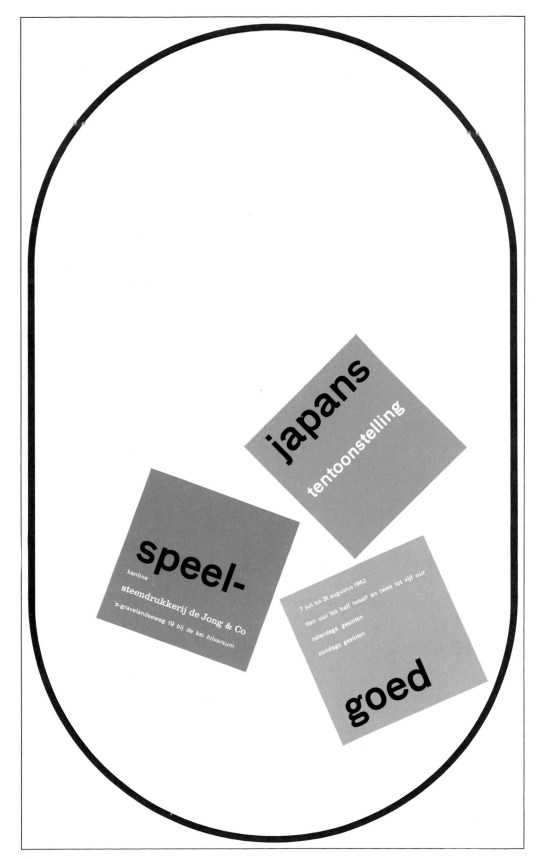

A programme of smells, 1965, see also page 151

This was not an exhibition but a programme during which, at certain hours, different smells were introduced into neutral surroundings.

design: Pieter Brattinga

een programma van geuren

10.00 uur: sinaasappel
11.00 uur: potlood
pauze
14.00 uur: anijs
15.00 uur: muskus

a programm of smells

10.00 hrs: orange
11.00 hrs: pencil
intermission
14.00 hrs: anise
15.00 hrs: musk

un programme d'odeurs

10.00 heures: orange
11.00 heures: crayon
entracte
14.00 heures: anis
15.00 heures: musc

ein programm von düften

10.00 uhr: apfelsine
11.00 uhr: bleistift
pause
14.00 uhr: anis
15.00 uhr: moschus

16 augustus tot 22 september 1965
10.00-11.30/14.00-17.00 uur
zaterdags en zondags gesloten

kantine
steendrukkerij de Jong & Co
printers, imprimeurs, drucker / offset-lithographic
's-gravelandseweg 19, hilversum, holland

What I like: Paul Huf, 1964, see also page 139

Poster for an exhibition of photographs by the internationally known Dutch photographer Paul Huf.

design: Pieter Brattinga

7 november tot 30 december 1964
10.00-11.30/14.00-17.00 uur
zaterdags en zondags gesloten

tentoonstelling

kantine
steendrukkerij de Jong & Co
printers, imprimeurs, drucker / offset-lithographic
's-gravelandseweg 19, hilversum, holland

.... wat ik mooi vind: paul huf

Iron sculpture, drawings and graphics by Carel Visser, 1959, see also page 125

Poster announcing an exhibition of work by the Dutch sculptor Carel Visser.

design: Pieter Brattinga.

ijzerplastiek, tekeningen en grafiek van carel visser

tentoonstelling

28 maart tot 4 mei

tien uur tot half twaalf en twee tot vijf uur

zaterdags tien uur tot half twaalf

zondags gesloten

kantine

steendrukkerij de Jong & Co

's-gravelandseweg 19 bij de kei hilversum

Nippon Design Center, 1963, see also page 149

Poster for an exhibition of designs by the Japanese advertising agency and studio, which was opened by Joseph Müller Brockman and attended by the members of the Alliance Graphique Internationale.

design: Pieter Brattinga

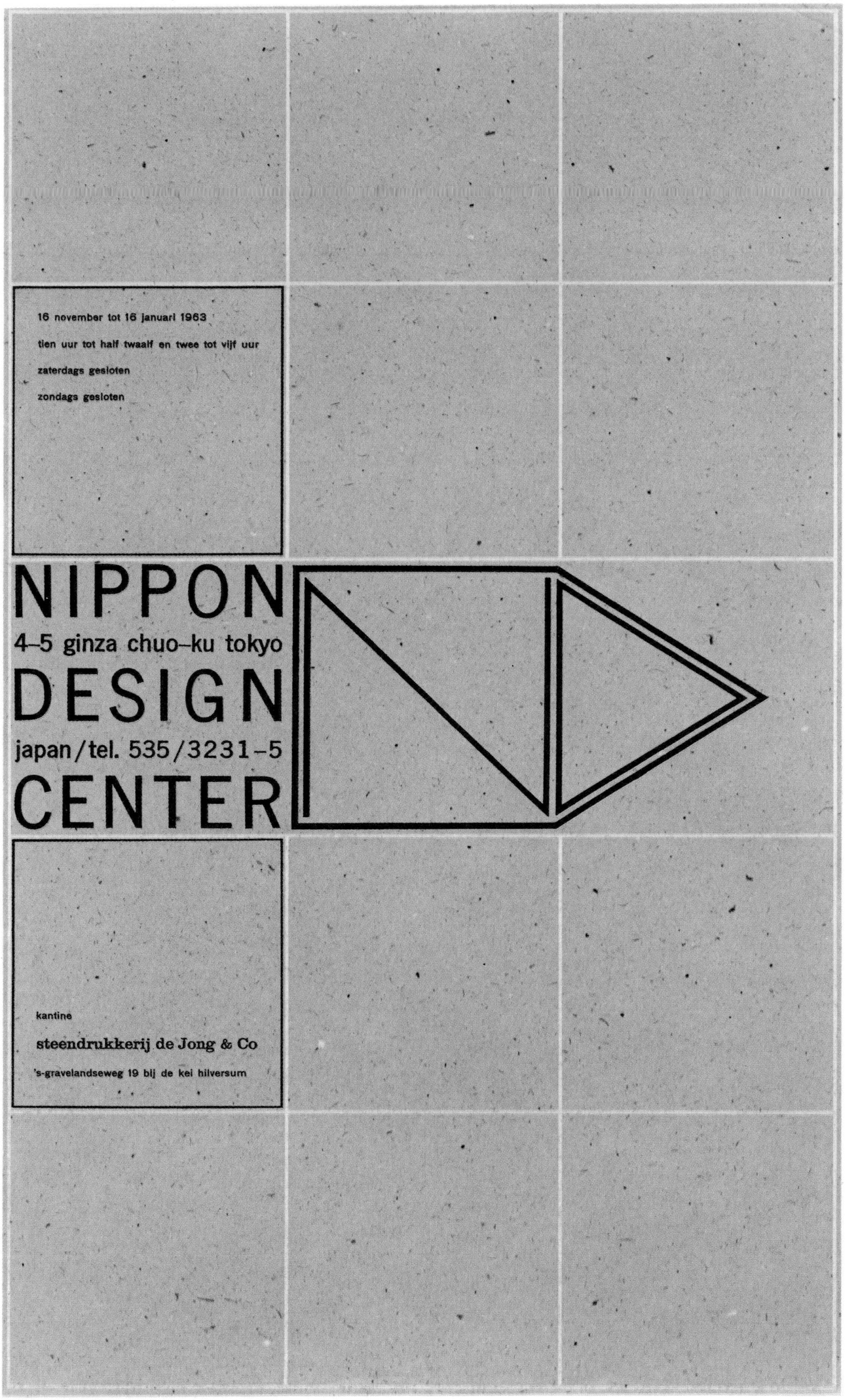

16 november tot 16 januari 1963

tien uur tot half twaalf en twee tot vijf uur

zaterdags gesloten

zondags gesloten

NIPPON

4–5 ginza chuo–ku tokyo

DESIGN

japan/tel. 535/3231–5

CENTER

kantine

steendrukkerij de Jong & Co

's-gravelandseweg 19 bij de kei hilversum

Drawings by Henk Broer, 1957

Poster for an exhibition of drawings by the Dutch artist Henk Broer.

design: Pieter Brattinga

tentoonstelling

tekeningen van henk broer

4 mei tot 5 juni

tien uur tot half twaalf en twee tot vijf uur

zaterdags tien uur tot half twaalf

zondags gesloten

kantine

steendrukkerij de Jong & Co

's-gravelandseweg 19 bij de kei hilversum

Typography Piet Zwart, 1960, see also page 145

Poster announcing an exhibition of work by this Dutch pioneer in typography of the 1920s.

design: Pieter Brattinga

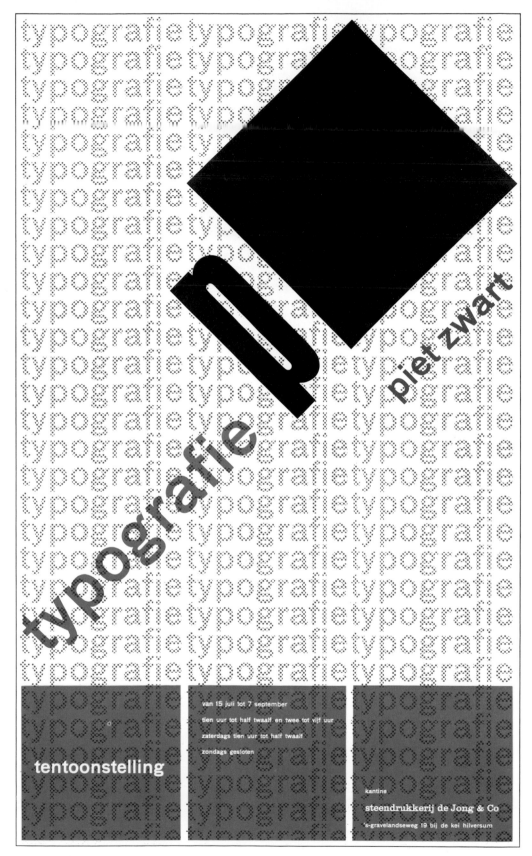

typografie

piet zwart

tentoonstelling

van 15 juli tot 7 september
tien uur tot half twaalf en twee tot vijf uur
zaterdags tien uur tot half twaalf
zondags gesloten

kantine
steendrukkerij de Jong & Co
's-gravelandseweg 19 bij de kei hilversum

105

A fashion designer for men: Alice Edeling

Poster for an exhibition about the work of a Dutch fashion designer.

design: Pieter Brattinga

zeven creatieve vrouwen
een serie tentoonstellingen

een mode-ontwerpster voor mannen: alice edeling

7 juli tot 31 augustus 1967
10.00-11.30/14.00-17.00 uur
zaterdags en zondags gesloten

tentoonstelling

kantine
steendrukkerij de Jong & Co
printers, imprimeurs, drucker / offset-lithographie
's-gravelandseweg 19, hilversum, holland

Ten years' education in typographic design, 1963

Poster for an exhibition showing the result of ten years of graphic design at the Amsterdam School of Applied Arts. Besides student and graduate work, the work of the two instructors, Melle and Charles Jongejans, was shown.

design: Pieter Brattinga

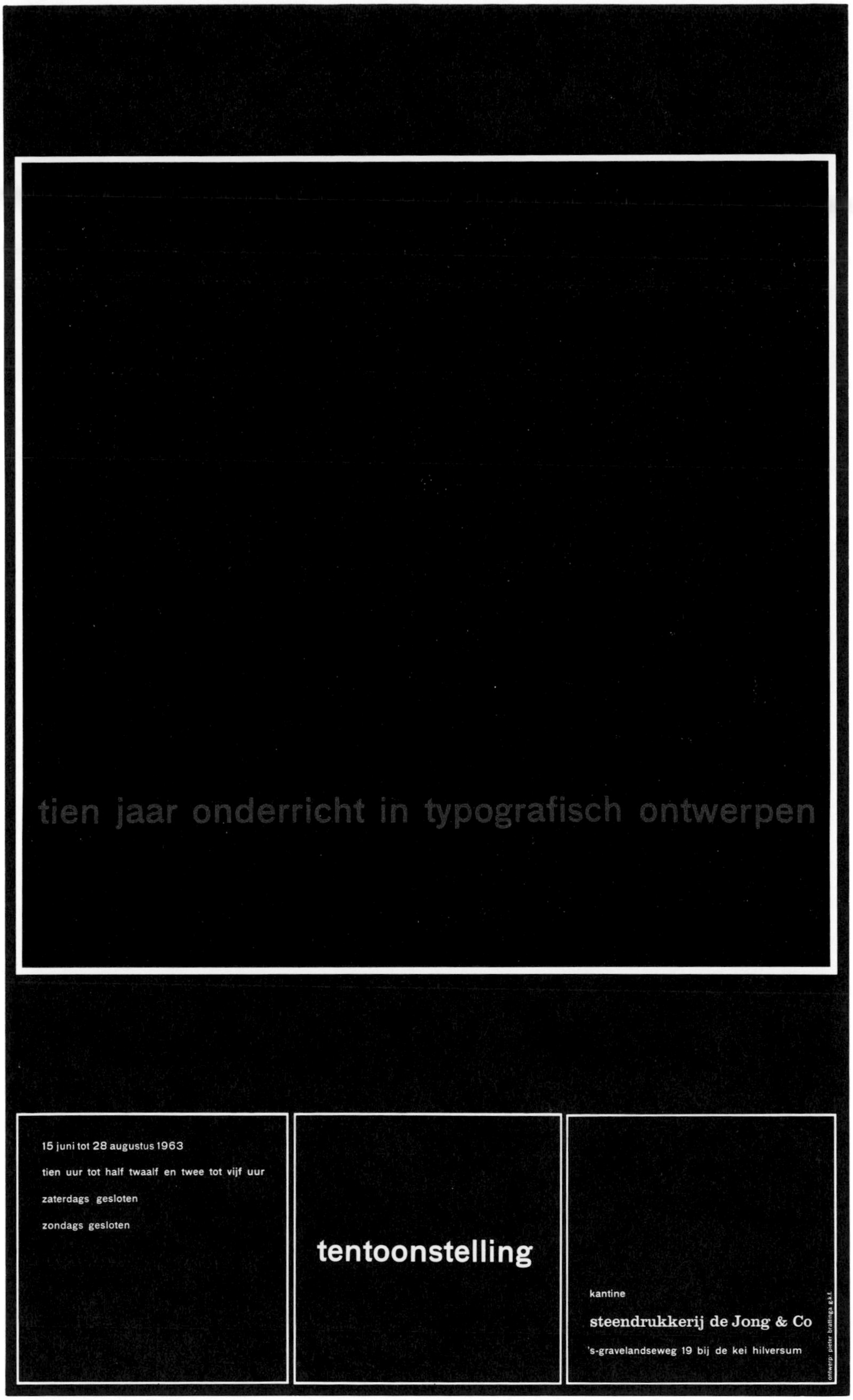

tien jaar onderricht in typografisch ontwerpen

15 juni tot 28 augustus 1963

tien uur tot half twaalf en twee tot vijf uur

zaterdags gesloten

zondags gesloten

tentoonstelling

kantine

steendrukkerij de Jong & Co

's-gravelandseweg 19 bij de kei hilversum

ontwerp pieter brattinga g.k.f

Four posters from a series 'seven creative women', 1967-1969

Top left: a decorator: Jehanne van Woerkom
Top right: a sculptress: Ferdi (horti-sculpture)
Bottom left: an industrial fashion–designer: Tine van Oosten
Bottom right: a poetess: F. Harmsen van Beek

design: Pieter Brattinga

zeven creatieve vrouwen
een serie tentoonstellingen

een versierster: jehanne van woerkom

tentoonstelling

steendrukkerij de Jong & Co

zeven creatieve vrouwen
een serie tentoonstellingen

een beeldhouwster: ferdi (hortisculpture)

tentoonstelling

steendrukkerij de Jong & Co

zeven creatieve vrouwen
een serie tentoonstellingen

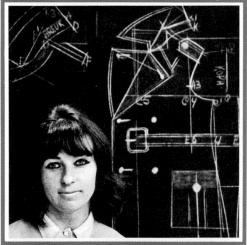

een industrieel mode-ontwerpster: tine van oosten

tentoonstelling

steendrukkerij de Jong & Co

zeven creatieve vrouwen
een serie tentoonstellingen

een dichteres: f. harmsen van beek

tentoonstelling

steendrukkerij de Jong & Co

Exhibitions

In 1954, at Brattinga's suggestion, and under his direction, it was decided to hold exhibitions in the canteen of steendrukkerij de Jong & Co. These were conceived originally as a social service for the workers who used the canteen and as a support for the arts. An opening statement pledged that in order to do this, work of the sponsor would never be shown. The shows attracted the attention of a wider audience and after the third exhibition they were opened to the general public. In 1957, the Pictura Prize of the Royal Academy of the Hague was awarded to the company with the citation 'through these exhibitions the public and your workers get acquainted with the best examples of international art, while your non-commercial publications, the Quadrat Prints, are of a perfect typographic design and a high literary standard'.
The gallery was redesigned in 1958 by Wim Crouwel and Kho Liang le, and a new series of exhibitions was mounted, beginning with the typography of Sandberg.
The exhibitions are avantgarde and aim to introduce the work of artists in all fields of modern art, especially young and unknown artists. Apart from displays or work by painters, sculptors, graphic designers, photographers and architects, the series has included 'a programme of smells', a collection of art nouveau vases and 'such Dadaistic gestures on occasion as inviting a large attendance to a Christmas party-cum-exhibition which proved to consist of three men eating a gargantuan meal inaccessibly on the far side of a glass wall'. (Architectural Review, London, August 1961).
Quite regularly artists such as Carel Visser and Tajiri, who have since gained a worldwide reputation, were given their first one-man show in the Gallery and were subsequently invited to show their work in Amsterdam's museum of modern art, the Stedelijk Museum. In 1960 a scoop was achieved when Pop Art was on show for the first time in the Netherlands.
Brattinga is determined that it will remain an experimental gallery rather than a show case for the work of established artists, and he is always open to new ideas for exhibitions. The exhibitions have attracted press attention in all parts of the world and have helped to give Hilversum the reputation of being a cultural centre in the Netherlands.

. . . these exhibitions cover a variety of subjects connected with graphics, photography and architecture as well as the fine arts, and are marked by great originality in choice of subject matter and display technique . . .

From Architectural Review, London, England, August 1961.

. . . Different designers and architects make memorable use of this very small room with a few square feet of garden outside. The thought and love put into these minute exhibitions, like the Quadrat Prints, have repercussions all over the world, reproduced and discussed in the most discerning magazines.

From 'Design coordination and corporate image' by F. H. K. Henrion and Alan Parkin, Studio Vista, London, England, 1967.

. . . Its success is another victory of good ideas and design policies.
From 'Graphic Design', Tokyo, Japan, July, 1962.

. . . Brattinga developed a plan of cooperation which had some fascinating results for various artists and also for himself. His initiatives for interesting exhibitions attracted much attention and gave food for discussion. Young artists are just as much at home there as the sandwich-eating workers and the inhabitants of Hilversum, who come to see the creations of their contemporaries. Not only from nearby but also from abroad, many have found their way to this resolutely directed art centre . . .

From the introduction by Sandberg. Catalogue/number 321 Stedelijk Museum, Amsterdam, Netherlands. 1963.

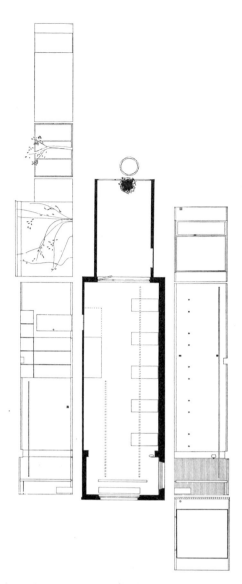

114

conway.

An exhibition of the typography of Sandberg, Albert Schulze Vellinghausen

The handwritten and typographic 'Experimenta' by Sandberg, a friend and fellow-warrior of Rietveld's, are on show. For the first time he has brought out his manifold typographic studies, designs and sketches. What emanates from these is of a more permanent nature than his catalogues and posters, and shows the mastership of his meditative and demonstrative ordering of the environment.
Even those who know him as director of the Amsterdam Stedelijk Museum, will be surprised not only by the clearness of his writings but by their fervour. It is made possible to cast a glance at the facts and be confronted with an activity which first of all disciplines itself, and then radiates outwards. The condition for hitting the mark in the first place is asceticism. The next step – just as with Rietveld – leads directly to spanning the world.

'Frankfurter Algemeine Zeitung', Frankfurt, Germany; June 2nd, 1959
design exhibition: Kho Liang Ie and Wim Crouwel

Sandberg

117

Sculptures by Tajiri, M. Visser

. . . As one enters the hall this time it is hard to suppress one's surprise, as one sees the collection of thin, seemingly fragile, but actually extremely strong bronze sculptures made by Tajiri. This American-born Japanese has been living in Holland for some years now, and has greatly influenced a number of Dutch sculptors.

Almost all the statuary on exhibition represents growth in the vegetable world, germination of the seed, sprouting upwards between the seed-lobes, roots pressing downwards into the earth. As children we have all mused over the marvel of the sprouting of a bean grown on a damp bit of sponge. This marvel of nature, this primitive force of life in the very smallest organism, this constant motion, Tajiri wished to portray, and has in fact reproduced. But if he had only reproduced the shapes as the eye perceives them, he would probably not have reached higher than a model for a lesson in botany.

Tajiri only gives an indication of the shapes by means of fine blades of bronze or thin bronze plates which he welds together and every weld, a little glossier than the material, is like a stage in the growth, a jump into life, a short interval in the development from seed to plant, where the sap of life flows onward. In this small light hall I have felt life vibrate around me, heard it rushing, and I have understood that the man who knows how to express this is a great and pure artist. . .

'De Waarheid', Amsterdam, Netherlands; August 1959
design exhibition: Wim Crouwel

An exhibition of art nouveau vases

'A phase in vases' 1895-1925, Willemijn Brattinga-Kooy
Living on a dike in a Dutch polder, two horizons are yours, one in front of your house, one behind it; it gives you a sense of space.
Pieter Groot collects Art Nouveau pottery for his friend, designer Alexander (Peter) Verberne.
Alexander only desires the perfect, which leaves a somewhat surprised Pieter the owner of a beautiful, damaged, hurt but not dead, piece of pottery. Suddenly he is a collector himself.
Rummaging around Amsterdam's fleamarket on the Waterlooplein and various small, out-of-the-way shops, please-Sir-take-it-with-you-I've-had-it-for-fifteen-years, he assembles a rather arbitrary collection until he happens to lay his hands on a slender trade booklet. Names such as Rozenburg, Mobach, Bergen op Zoom, de Distel, Amstelhoek, Colenbrander, van der Hoef, Serf, de Lorm, Lanooy and Nienhuis and their factory markings and signatures have no secrets for him any more. . .

From the catalogue, 1965
design exhibition: Pieter Brattinga

119

Political cartoons and drawings by Opland

A long row of long-nosed, fat-stomached, hollow-eyed creatures, all distorted and enlarged, leads
you along the way to the canteen entrance. The best Dutch cartoonist and caricaturist is showing
his work here. A great man, Opland, with practically unlimited creative abilities which express
themselves in a curious way: very heavy outlines, seemingly childish presentations, and a
tendency for defending the weak. In the course of years he has made caricatures for such Dutch
newspapers as 'De Volkskrant' 'De Groene' and 'Het Parool', and when we stop to consider
we realize how few good cartoonists there are in this country. Like the long deceased Albert Hahn,
this political cartoonist distorts important and dignified people with relentless ferocity and a
inborn sense of humour. Figures such as General de Gaulle, Dr. Luns, General Eisenhower are
ridiculed to the absurd in this lashing of our petty-bourgeois complacency.

'De Volkskrant', Amsterdam, Netherlands; September 14th, 1959
design exhibition: Charles Jongejans

Introduction by
poet Simon Vinkenoog

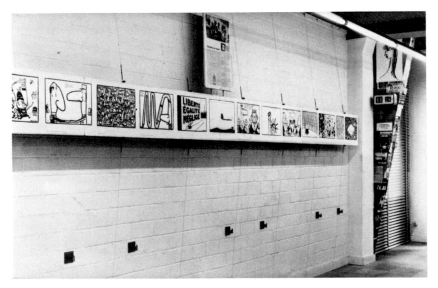

An exhibition of collages by John McHale and Cornelius Bastiaan Vaandrager.

Print – tear + form = picture.
Hilversum – Many pounds of glue and paste have been used in the preparation of the exhibition Print-minus-tear-plus-form-equals-picture, which shows collages by the Glasgow painter John McHale (37) and the Rotterdam poet Cornelius Bastiaan Vaandrager (24). Collages could most easily be described as 'artistic pastings'.
The Japanese artist Tajiri who had been asked to arrange the exhibition, also made it into an artistic 'pasting': he cut and glued together the large, light blue airmail paper in which the exhibition is being held.
This 'tent' has a curious influence on visitors. Those who wish to see the collages are forced first to make a humble bow for them (the entrance is low); the delicate, fragile paper surroundings tend to hold this humble attitude and preserve it. People dare not raise their voices.
We believe this is the best atmosphere to digest Vaandrager's collages. They seem so simple: words from newspapers, sometimes complete sentences have been cut, re-cut and pasted by Vaandrager. Complete 'poems' have been produced that forcibly strike the perceptive faculties of the reader (viewer?). Words the average newspaper reader devours by the hundred, words becoming worn out – these same words have gained new force. Vaandrager knows how to express his fear for these times – which may or may not be modish – poetically in this way.
McHale cut up coloured pictures and pasted them into paintings, which – where composition and colour are concerned – are pure beauty.

'Algemeen Dagblad', Rotterdam, Netherlands; April, 1960
design exhibition: Tajiri

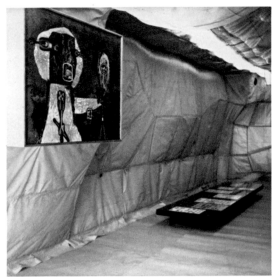

Rietveld

123

Sculptures by Carel Visser, Albert Schulze Vellinghausen

Young German sculptors are becoming increasingly interested in the reconnoitering of broken
structures. What they discover there marks the face of our present-day exhibitions, not least
in the comprehensive balance which the 'Kunstverein Hannover' wishes to show under the title
'The New Generation'. Sometimes it even is a new kind of Rococo – in bronze, stainless steel and
other metals – making the most of the charm of the material.
That, contrary to this delight in 'romantic' ebullition, it is also possible to remain true to harder
constructivism, and to modify it, may be proved by the sculptures of our 'rationalistic'
neighbours, the young Dutchmen. Among them – as could be observed at the Brussels 'Expo' –
Carel Visser is continually gaining in importance. He wrests more and more figurative elements
from his hard wrought iron, in a reliable, slow, but very convincing way. The collection emphatically
points to this thirty year old – an elementary force . . .

Frankfurter Algemeine Zeitung, Frankfurt, Germany; April 1959
design exhibition: Kho Liang Ie

An exhibition of wood type, Willemijn Brattinga-Kooy

The man who assembled these pieces of wood type painstakingly assembled a remarkable piece
of Americana.
His name is Rob Roy Kelly; a darkhaired, intense Irish American, he has a passion for traditional
wood type to which he owes a collection of sleek, blackish, dark-hard type faces. This collection
stored away alphabet by alphabet in countless dusty boxes, fills his room, his house almost,
stacked to the ceiling.
In snow and storm, sun and heat, driving his stationwagon like a determined dachshund, Kelly
follows the roads of the Midwest, Maine, Vermont and New York State, through the old sleepy
towns, where dust and mud are yellow and Pete around the corner sells firearms, searching for the
small printshops, hoping they will sell him old type.
For hours he talks shop with the printers, and these men, who have handled the type for so many
years and occasionally have changed the old ornaments according to their own wishes, whose
fingers now blindly, surely touch the hard velvety wood, finally agree to sell.

From the catalogue, January 1965
design exhibition: Pieter Brattinga

124

An exhibition of drawings, paintings and photographs of eyes

Eyes Opened at Exhibition on Looking
Carel Blazer has made eye-catching enlargements of portraits from journals – often including the
'grain'. They are the direct eye-catchers of the exhibition 'Looking' showing reprints of advertise-
ments in which the human eye is displayed in some way.
As an example of exhibition art, this exclusive show, by architect Kho Liang Ie and designer
Gerard Wernars, is certainly worth seeing.
Simon Vinkenoog took the floor, from which an eye squinted at him. Vinkenoog appeared to have
busied himself with books, full of pages of play upon words with 'eye', 'looking' and 'seeing'.
A subject upon which this original speaker, with a glint of pleasure in his eye, had been pleased to
cast his eyes.
The regular visitors to the Steendrukkerij's canteen opened their eyes wide to view the
exhibition and their mouths to drink the traditional glass of white wine, which in my eyes, is yellow.

'Het Vrije Volk', Amsterdam, Netherlands; May 27th, 1961
design exhibition: Kho Liang Ie and Gerard Wernars

An exhibition of paintings by Karl Gerstner

Quadratic 'Art' by Karl Gerstner, Jan P. Koenraads
Whether the art exhibited by Karl Gerstner can be qualified as art in the usual sense, will no
doubt remain a disputed question.
He starts out from the square, the pure diagonal section within it and the circle. The result is a
purely geometrical relief in metal or glass.
... It is exactly this renouncing of the soul – the always imperfect human emotion – of these
strictly dogmatic, and from a material point of view perfect creations, which mark it as a
phenomenon that has nothing to do with art.
These imperfections inherent in the human soul, activate imagination and leave space for a
supposed perfection of the representation. Gerstner does not leave this space. What he does is
concrete, correct and justified in every respect. He is the renouncer of all values outside or above
the materially comprehensible and therefore not subject to reason.
He is the 'almost' perfect antipode of an artist; almost, because in this world nothing will ever be
perfect, not even the too concrete art of Karl Gerstner.

'Het Vrije Volk', Amsterdam, Netherlands; June 27th, 1964
design exhibition: Wim Crouwel

126

An exhibition of publicity design for the Hessischer Rundfunk (Hesse Radio Corporation) and the Columbia Broadcasting System

German & American Graphic Design on show at de Jong's, James Moran.
All graphic design for the Hesse organization (Hessischer Rundfunk) is prepared by Hans Michel and Günther Kieser (Novum Group). The art director is E. Rolf Richter and his assistant is Richard Weigand.
Graphic design for the American organization, Columbia Broadcasting System, is directed and designed by art director Louis Dorfsman. The graphic material of CBS is primarily directed to selling transmitting time to industry. Advertising material is also supplied to the network of stations (203 in number) for use locally. Finally CBS aims a portion of its advertising to the public.

From 'Printing News', London, England; June 1959
design exhibition: Wim Crouwel

---

500 Paperback covers by Dick, H. v.d. Horst

'500 Covers by Dick' was the title of an exhibition arranged to celebrate the publication of the 500th 'Zwarte Beertjes' paperback ... On inspection of the covers it will be evident that Dick Bruna is a master in the art of omission ...

'Nieuwsblad voor de Boekhandel', Amsterdam, Netherlands; June 1st, 1962
design exhibition: Gerard Wernars

129

Spiritual Opening of Photo Exhibition, Theo Ramaker

'Man in Moscow' at de Jong's of Hilversum.
The exhibition 'Man in Moscow' by photographer Eddy Posthuma de Boer was opened as if it
were a worldexhibition. Actually there were only some forty photographs on view, showing no
more than a limited aspect of the Russian capital.
In view of the small space available in the fine gallery, Posthuma de Boer and his advisers had
decided to show only the people of Moscow. As such it was a good collection, fortunately giving
quite a different picture of these people from the photos referred to by the 'official opener' of the
exhibition, Ed van der Elsken, as 'the Kolynos girls on clean tractors, the soldiers marching in
their ranks and the workers walking in the streets reading Dostoievsky, as found in Russian
journals'.
What made the opening so impressive was the fact that the whole of the Federation of Applied
Artists had shown up, and that a multitude of friends, many prominent artists and journalists, and
also two representatives of the Russian Embassy in the Hague had come. The latter listened very
attentively to the frank speech van der Elsken made, from which we quote: 'What you see here is
not the spontaneous work of a western individualist, grown up in an atmosphere of free expression.
No, it is directed work decreed by the state. Posthuma de Boer was commissioned to make this
series of photographs via the Russian Embassy's secret service, and he was instructed to give a
sombre, threatening picture of the Soviet Union and its inhabitants'.
Some of those present found it somewhat difficult to recognize that van der Elsken was joking
when he continued: 'What inspired this curious behaviour of the Russians? Although they perform
fantastic feats in the fields of economy and science, the average Dutchman still looks upon a
Russian as something that came crawling out from under a stone. Uncle Sam, on the contrary,
discovered that those showing their faults and foibles suggest hidden power. In the States,
according to van der Elsken 'they even go as far as to accentuate negative aspects to such a degree
that modern public opinion interprets these as proofs of strength. Shortly we shall also see more
optimistic work by the Russians too, which will be indistinguishable from Tabu'.
Finally, where the exhibition is concerned, the designers have made an especially effective entrance
with the picture of crowds entering the small hall. However no small demands are made on the
litheness of visitors who come to examine pictures hung about an inch from the floor.

'Het Parool', Amsterdam, Netherlands; July 17th, 1961
design exhibition: Wim Crouwel and Gerard Wernars

A celebration exhibition after five years of exhibitions.

Come dine with me artificially
'. . (because it) was desired to celebrate this fact (the 5 – year anniversary of exhibitions) in a very
special way, an exhibition entitled 'Art-ificial food' was organized . . . wooden hams – plaster
sorbets, foam rubber pastries taken from the butchers' and bakers' shop-window . . . made your
mouth water . . . suddenly the visitors saw behind a lighted window an exquisitely laid table with
three men around it, digging into an enormous turkey and washing it down with quantities of
wine. The angry grumbling of the hungry crowd was interrupted by a speech by cartoonist Opland
which was the sign for a few waiters to feed the crowd a series of weird looking victuals – blue
eggs, bread with red, green and yellow creamcheese and poison-coloured drinks . . .

'Volkskrant', Amsterdam, Netherlands; February 29th, 1960
design exhibition and murals: Jan Bons

An exhibition of rubbings of manhole covers from New York, Hans Redeker

An exhibition of manhole covers from the streets of New York is a relishing subject for subtle reflections on modern man in the streets, who walks mechanically over a world that is non-existent to him because he does not notice it.
An underworld of sewers, water mains and gas pipes, together just as essential to his existence as his own blood circulation or metabolism, to this world the manhole covers are the entrance and symbol. The conclusion of such reflections is the necessity of making people see things in a new light and calling attention to them by means of creative action. Thus we arrive at Pop Art.
In this case it would have been more effective to exhibit the manhole covers themselves. Transferred as a kind of letterpress printing on a neat surface and in a well-considered composition, they are in fact already estranged from themselves, they have become esthetic and decorative, confectionery for commercial designers and window-dressers. The only thing to do is to open up the sewers of Hilversum and go down in them yourself, because at this exhibition too little that feeds the relationship between this underworld and our subconscious comes to light.

'Algemeen Handelsblad', Amsterdam, Netherlands; September 5th, 1964
design exhibition: Pieter Brattinga

Japanese Toys

Oh, it's only a show
Bamboo chickens, cats and spinning little Japanese
In an atmosphere of curiosity and tenderness 6 Japanese children dressed in flapping kimonos and clattering around on high wooden sandals hoisted festive paper fishes to the top of a high mast in the garden, and thus opened an exhibition of Japanese toys. At Brattinga's request a Japanese friend and colleague, Hiroshi Ohchi, went into a department store to buy all the toys he thought would please the non-Japanese eye. Designers Gerard Wernars and Kho Liang Ie were delighted to display the many-coloured fantastic surprises on cardboard shelves.
Japanese Embassy children, Hoshie, Yukio, Akiko, Miwako and Kumiko, accompanied by their smiling, silently filming parents, added charm to the proceedings. When asked whether the children in Japan enjoy playing with these toys, the oldest Japanese child (7) answered: 'Oh no, it's only a show'.

'Haagse Post', Amsterdam, Netherlands; July 21st, 1962
design exhibition: Kho Liang Ie and Gerard Wernars

Exhibition: form and aerial photograph, Sandberg

From an aeroplane we see shapes below us, and above us cloud masses lighten or darken the cloud-cover underneath like a cottonwool blanket. Sometimes there are strangely shaped holes through which parts of the surface of the earth become visible, like a pattern, and then again like irregular stains on a damp cellar wall.
And I often think, possibly because I am in contact with them every day, that they are like paintings, statues, graphic art.
Maybe the reason for this is that all shapes can be reduced to a limited number of types.
Types, which nature makes use of, man when dividing a plot of land, and the artist who tries to give shape to his ideas on a rectangular panel, in wrought iron, or stone.

From the catalogue; 1960
design exhibition: Pieter Brattinga

A Game of Cards

Now and again all of us have cast an eye at the devil's picture book. Who doesn't play a game of cards sometimes? What we seldom pause to consider while we are playing bridge, whist or canasta is that our pack of cards has had a stormy past, in which it broke hearts, reduced people to beggary, and was in league with politics. During the French revolution, for instance, all kings and queens on playing cards were replaced by 'sages' and 'virtues' and the jack became a republican with a liberty cap. Who would ever have thought that in former days men were branded and sent to the galleys as a punishment for making 'contraband' cards? Once a man was even hanged for forging an ace . . .
Card games are age-old and international. We know Indian, Chinese, Korean, Japanese, Italian, German and French playing cards. This exhibition of a small but colourful selection was introduced in an unusual manner by Henk van der Horst, director of the Committee for Promotion of the Dutch Book. He illustrated a special aspect of card games, conjuring tricks with cards. For this occasion he had practised a number of tricks which he demonstrated with precise explanations . . .
It was not the intention to give a chronological survey, but only a superficial impression of various forms and uses of old and modern playing cards. Renaissance, Biedermeier and Mexican cards, Majong, Tarok and fortune-teller's cards, Rosicrucian and political cards were on display, together with modern cards, some designed by the Swiss Honneger Lavater and the Frenchman Jean Piccard Le Doux.

'De Volkskrant', Amsterdam, Netherlands; September 1964
design exhibition: Wim Crouwel and Gerard Wernars

Photographs by Paul Huf, Dick Dooyes

'Paul Huf is a poetic stage-director who turns situations into songs. His photographs give evidence of people and say things to people. Goethe's pronouncement that every good poem is an occasional poem, can be applied to Paul Huf's photos: servitude to the community is the point of departure of his work. Their attraction lies in the magic influence evoked by the photographer, based on flawless rendering of matter, which might be termed the *vox humana* of pictorial art. Seventeenth century painting demonstrates how much rendering of texture is an essentially national characteristic of Dutch art'. This is a very concise summary of an opinion expressed by Professor Dr. H. van de Waal, Director of the Gallery of Prints of the State University of Leyden, in his introduction to the exhibition of work by Paul Huf. The large audience listened attentively to this absorbing speech – the tension, however, relaxed for a moment when the shrill cry of a child sounded through the crowded hall just as the speaker pronounced the words *'vox humana'*. That childish sound was like the accent given by a vivid dab of colour in an otherwise sober composition, and it reminded me of one of the many beautiful colour transparencies on show. It is a publicity photograph for Le Monde: a small inner court with the silhouette of a cat on a gate. Apart from his attention to the human element and the flawless expression of texture, this is a third important quality in Huf's work: colour composition. This is often used with the utmost refinement in his work for extensive advertising campaigns.
Paul Huf – son of an accomplished actor of the same name – is widely known. The small exhibition, composed with great care and beautifully arranged, offers a unique opportunity to become acquainted more intimately, with this Dutch photographer of international stature.
Willemijn Brattinga-Kooy quotes Paul Huf in her 'Portrait of a Photographer' printed in the 'Lilliput-Quadrat Print' for the exhibition: 'Actually all my photos are portraits, in the sense that they are essentials of the subjects commissioned. When such a subject is reduced to essentials not only the photograph comes across, but the message behind it as well'.

'Drukkersweekblad', Amsterdam, Netherlands; December 4th, 1965
design exhibition: Wim Crouwel

An exhibition of pages from the magazine: Architectural Review

The AR was shown partly in mosaics of pasted-up pages on the walls, and partly in suspended rings containing a selection of typical REVIEW covers from the post-war years. The exhibition was opened by the Dutch graphic designer Juriaan Schrofer, and with a lecture by the architect Hein Salomonson, which gives an interesting picture of the image of the AR which is entertained in some quarters:
'It is tempting to go into its typically English character, but I don't think that it is at all necessary. Each number begins with a general subject, as general as possible, which shows – quite justly – how catholic an architect's range of interest and ideas must be and can be.
You might find an article by some chap who has driven right across the USA and hardly mentions architecture . . . In AR there is a frequently recurring discussion, the point of which escapes me, on New Brutalism. Among the many positive comments I have to make, I should like to mention one thing I have objection to: it is especially easy, in this general section, to take a high-handed attitude. It is my belief that we architects are right in being unwilling to exaggerate, and in drawing comparisons based on New Brutalism, AR seems to me to go too far in this respect . . .
It is very remarkable how these very critical, outspoken and pungent articles are usually followed by one or more architectural works; these are topical, sometimes – it is true – accompanied by criticism, but it is a good thing the choice isn't too fastidious. The editors just show us what is being made at the moment and add their comments . . .'
Sharp-eyed readers, who examine the photographs closely, will see that de Jong's choice was not too fastidious either, and included the kind of article to which Salomonson objected, as well as those he approved.

Architectural Review, London, England; August, 1961
design exhibition: Benno Wissing

Genius Discovered, Lambert Tegenbosch

A resident of The Hague whose attitude towards reality is very strange is Willem van Genk, whom J. J. Beljon, Director of the Royal Academy of Arts of The Hague, emphatically acclaims as a discovery and a genius.

A few years ago van Genk presented himself to Mr. Beljon to learn to paint. But the Director of the Academy recognized immediately that van Genk's abilities did not fit in with the didactic possibilities of his school, and he placed him in the evening class where he let him do as he liked.

The works of this lonely van Genk are views of towns. They are pen drawings filled in with colours. It is not necessary for him to have seen the towns to be able to draw them. He documents himself meticulously, becomes obsessed by the town (Moscow, Cologne, Tokyo, Paris, Antwerp, Leipzig, Amsterdam, The Hague, Arnhem), and sometimes can work for years on a bird's-eye-view of such a town. A beautiful specimen is the large view of Moscow. To see this is to understand Beljon's enthusiasm.

Beljon's convincing introduction of van Genk's work states among other things: 'in one of the most delightful autobiographies I know, namely that of Man Ray, one can read that Man Ray, after he had lived in Paris for over twenty years, ventured for the first time into the Louvre. He was out again within half an hour. Man Ray is a great artist in contrast to the thousands who have made the contents of the Louvre their own spiritual property'.

... It is a fact that neither the Academy nor the Museum can create artists. Both, however, may be valuable to born artists, and in general, 'art' has been of no mean value for the development of artists. That van Genk cannot be approached by art, is possibly the reason why his work starts to oppress in the long run: his is a talent definitely not to be underestimated, but which still appears to be doomed to demonstrate itself in repetition, which possibly will not allow further growth. On these grounds, comparison with the customs officer Rousseau seems inadmissible ...

'De Volkskrant', Amsterdam, Netherlands; February 1st, 1964
design exhibition: G. Wernars

An exhibition of designs by Piet Zwart
An exhibition of Pioneer Work, Dick Dooyes

A retrospective exhibition of Zwart's work was opened by Karl Gerstner, a young designer from Basel. From his interesting introduction – a warm homage by a young artist from abroad to a Dutch pioneer – I am pleased to quote a few fragments:
'We consider many things to be a matter of course, and in an era in which so much stress is laid on public communication this may appear to be so, but essentially it is not true. Or don't you consider an exhibition of printed matter produced some ten, twenty, thirty or more years ago for a certain accurately defined purpose as something extraordinary? These prints in themselves do not even have any commercial value. No, they are more or less accidentally preserved copies of letterpaper, publicity folders, advertisements, that have outlived their time . . . But still they interest us because they are Piet Zwart's work . . .
Comparing Zwart to the architect Rietveld (who also attended the introduction ceremony) Gerstner said: 'Just think of his (Rietveld's) famous red and blue chair of 1918 and compare this with some of Zwart's advertisements for the 'Kabelfabrieken'. What wood and wood joints are for Rietveld, the typographic elements and their combinations are for Zwart. In both cases, but in different fields, material and construction were restricted inexorably and with an almost obsessive honesty to the most elementary. Their monumental value was understood and experienced as beauty. To have discovered this was doubtless an act of historical importance. Now, we can hardly imagine that at the time it was considered abnormal to place a line of print vertically on a page, to work with thick lines, to make white on black part of the composition . . .'
Gerstner pointed out that Zwart treated photography in the same revolutionary manner: 'his work ranges from almost scientific, strictly business-like pictures to photo-montages brimful of ideas – always in accordance with the appointed task. By means of contrasts in significance and forms he produces tension, he combines various perspectives and uses different scales for various elements in one picture. Where he finds this effective he makes use of negative images, he works with photographs (that are) cut up, distorted or silhouetted . . .'

'Drukkersweekblad', Amsterdam, Netherlands; July 1960
design exhibition: Wim Crouwel

Piet Zwart and cigarette
Gerstner and Brattinga

An exhibition of corporate designs for the Canadian National Railways, Jan v. Keulen

... the representation of this (CNR) company must be on the same level as its technical development. Of course it has never been the intention to use the identification symbol designed by Allan Flemming as an exhibition subject ...

'De Groene Amsterdammer', Amsterdam, Netherlands; March 23rd, 1963
design exhibition: Gerard Wernars

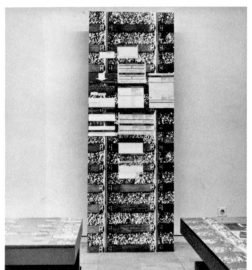

An exhibition of designs by the Nippon Design Center

International top graphic designers were tightly packed together in the narrow room, even the
Swiss designer Jozef Müller-Brockmann who introduced the exhibition of designs by the Nippon
Design Center, had no room to move. Advantage: there was no danger of his losing his balance.
All the big boys were there, Saul Bass who gained world fame through the design of titles for such
films as West Side Story, Anatomy of a Murder, Exodus and The Man with the Golden Arm.
Famous designer of children's books, Jan Lenica, Walter Herdeg, publisher and editor of the
journal 'Graphis', prominent French poster-designer Jacques Nathan-Garamond, Grignani from
Milan, British, Swiss, a German, Swedes and the Dutchmen Crouwel, Brusse, Bons and Treumann.
And, of course, Jonkheer Sandberg. Professor Pieter Brattinga, on a visit from New York, had
invited this international company of participants in the Congress of the Alliance Graphique
Internationale in Amsterdam to Hilversum.
Müller-Brockmann, who appeared to have examined things accurately in Tokyo, disclosed that the
Nippon Design Center, a number of whose striking posters, advertisements and other designs
could be admired in the gallery, already constituted a cultural factor of importance, although it was
only established in the second half of 1960. Its foundation came about in a remarkable way. Two
years ago, the Japanese radio corporation interviewed an American graphic designer who had
been commissioned to devise a cigarette package for a Japanese firm, earning 35 thousand dollars
for the assignment. At the time the interviewer posed the question whether Japan itself had no
designers who could do the job just as well, and probably at a less prohibitive fee.
A captain of industry, also known in his country as an art collector, Maecenas, idealist, was so
impressed by this broadcast that he took the initiative for the foundation of a design center,
supported by designers and industry jointly on the principle of working in unison. A great number
of firms participated, and thus the Nippon Design Center came into existence, effectively backed
by eight huge enterprises . . .

'Gooi en Eemlander', Hilversum, Netherlands; November, 13th, 1962
design exhibition: Gerard Wernars

Schleger, Sandberg, Herdeg.   Schleger, Herdeg, Him.

Wetli, Piatti, Wirth,
Müller-Brockmann.

Zimmerman, Richez,
Mrs. Sandberg, Ifert,
Eckersley, Kinneir.

A program of smells
Olfactory Factory

At 23, Dutch artist Wim Schippers is already a dedicated Wizard of Odd. He has built a 30-foot-high, violet coloured easy chair in Amsterdam's main park and directed a 'happening' during which four nattily dressed gentlemen emptied a bottle of lemonade into the North Sea. But that was only busy-work.
Now Schippers has switched senses going, one might say, from pop art to proboscis art. This month, Schippers' 'Program of Smells' was pulling sniffs and snorts in the company canteen of de Jong lithographers, in the Dutch city of Hilversum.
To company artistic adviser Pieter Brattinga, a veteran patron of the avantgarde, Schippers sold the idea of building a large box-like room in which scent-lovers could sit, undistracted by sound or colour, and contemplate the deeper implication of such odours as orange, pencil, anise and musk.
Twitch: Lined with white paper and lighted by bare bulbs, the odour chamber is 35 feet long and contains twelve chairs. Pungent effusions begin daily at 10 a.m. with a new (synthetic) smell every hour. The first, orange, which Brattinga's wife, Willemijn, describes as 'produced with a Southern temperament' is followed by the 'deeper fragrance' of pencil, which pulls the mind's nose away from sunnier climes and back to 'memories of work, school and office'. After that, she says, 'winter pleasures are recalled by Schippers by his witty aroma of anise'.
Finally, the scentsational climax comes, as nostrils twitch under the onslaught of sultry musk, which, says Mme Brattinga, seemed to be 'familiar to many, though perhaps subconsciously'.
If Schippers is simply tweaking the nose of Corporate-Sponsored art, he will not say. But Brattinga judges that almost 1,000 people have sat and sniffed inside the olfactory factory. When one middle-aged visitor was asked to identify himself and describe his reactions, he replied: 'My name and occupation do not matter but I am a connoisseur of life and it feels good to be here'.

'Newsweek', New York, U.S.A.; September 20th, 1965
design exhibition: Pieter Brattinga

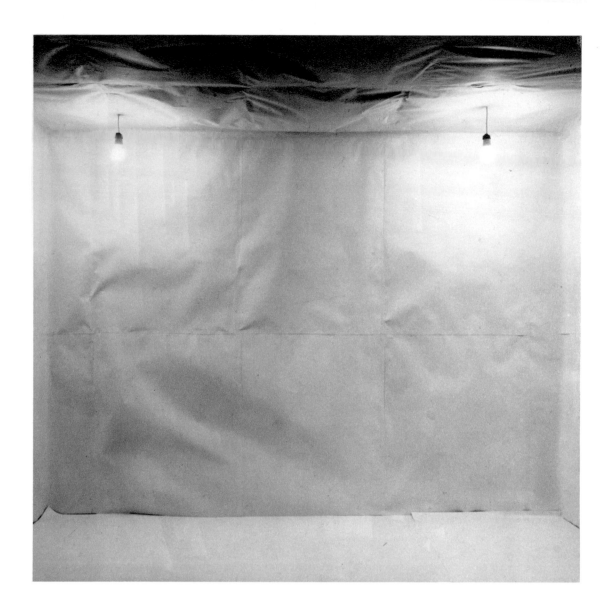

An exhibition of paintings by Daan van Golden
Art, C. Doelman

Perhaps he is like one of 'the poets who never penned'.

'Nieuwe Rotterdamsche Courant', Rotterdam, Netherlands; date unknown
design exhibition: Pieter Brattinga

An exhibition of Horti-sculpture by Ferdi Tajiri
Ferdi Tajiri, gardener in a dream garden.

She makes a whirling entry with a brush in her hand. In tight-fitting, small boots and under a blond wig, she click-clacked towards the exhibition hall: Ferdi (a first name like an opera) Tajiri. A small energetic woman who parks her VW bus like a truck driver . . . In the Series 'Seven Creative Women' Ferdi was the second, and with her 'Horti-sculpture' she brought many, often mini-skirted, colleagues.
Gas-stoves took sizzling care of a pleasant temperature. Nervous as a prima ballerina before her first 'swan' Ferdi tripped through the exhibition hall. She arranged some of her immense plants and flowers, brushed the long-haired body of her gigantic dragon-fly and corrected the position of its wings . . .

'De Gooi en Eemlander', Hilversum, Netherlands; Saturday May 6th, 1967
design exhibition: Pieter Brattinga

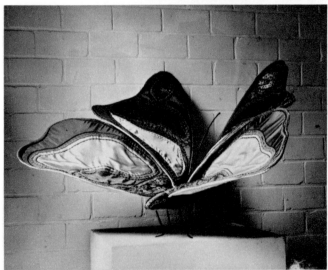

An exhibition of the work and surroundings of a poetess
Exhibition in a bedroom

It has often been argued that professional women are too rarely taken seriously. The legislature places women second, and for this reason it is being attempted, under the title 'Seven Creative Women', to give an insight into their work, their talent, their aims and their . . . backgrounds.
The first to be selected was the poetess Fr. Harmsen van Beek of Blaricum, who made her début in 1965 . . .
. . . Some of the poems of this volume are now exhibited on large placards. Her illustrations for the book are also shown . . .
. . . as far as we know this is a unique venture.
But it was not considered enough. Illustrate the poems – or rather furnish them – with something of the poetess's personality . . . Fritzi Harmsen van Beek had part of her home, that is her bedroom, moved to Steendrukkerij de Jong's canteen. When entering unsuspectingly to look at the poems one has the honour of seeing the paintress-poetess lying in bed . . . An old-fashioned high iron bedstead, painted black with brass knobbery, and all this under a rose and black wall-paper.
It is true that she does not lie there (that is her image in wax) during the entire exhibition, but still the bed situation is maintained as realistically as possible. Fritzi Harmsen van Beek can also be heard. The viewer-reader only has to press the button of a tape-recorder to be addressed by the deep – and on the tape also sweet – voice of the lady-poet.
. . . We must admit that we were impressed. We admire the initiative as far as it concerns the point of departure of 'Seven Creative Women'. But is there a need to have a *bed*? It is also possible to take originality too far! . . .

'Goois Nieuwsblad', Hilversum, Netherlands; March 13th, 1967
design exhibition: Pieter Brattinga

Planning for art

Planning for Art

Brattinga is interested in the new and experimental in art. No one can predict what form the art of the future will take. Developments in engineering, chemistry, physics, space exploration, have all had an effect on art that could not have been foreseen. The broader horizons of the artist today influence his work even if only subconsciously. Every new development is a challenge to him and will help to form his work, sometimes negatively in the form of rejection. For instance new alloys, new plastics, are constantly being produced and these stimulate the artist to find ways of benefitting from their properties, so affecting the form of the art produced. Each new medium imposes its limitations and this also influences the character of the work. Brattinga believes that art will widen its scope to include fields which are not now thought of as having any connection with art, and that formal divisions in the arts will become less important. As art comes to rely more on technical help, art and industry will cooperate more. Artists, with their more flexible minds, will contribute the ideas but industry will provide the means to realize them. But, just as technical problems involved in the realization may alter the idea of the artist and give an unexpected result, so technical discoveries made in the process may have commercial potential. Both sides will benefit from the interaction. If for example, movable coloured lights develop to replace conventional paintings the artist needs technical help to achieve his intentions. No longer can an artist be a man working on his own in a studio; artist and technicians will work together to develop an idea which will benefit them both, until the distinction between artist and technician will become less apparent.
Just as advances in engineering and sciences must constantly be put before the artist to stimulate him, so the public must be exposed to his work. By constant contact with new ideas the general public must be educated to use their own judgement. There are no absolute standards in art, it must be presented in such a way that everyone can form their own opinion. People must be pressed to experiment, to open their minds to what art has to offer them.

The living wall and fence, Pieter Brattinga

Years ago a respectable man bought a house on Muscle Beach.
Respectable as he was, he felt annoyed by the behaviour of sinful teenagers. The fence of verdure surrounding his house had to disappear, because he did not want to see or hear youth.
So the fence went and a wall came to take its place. A fine, smooth white wall that was wonderful to lean against.
The boys and girls took notice of this tacit rebuke, but they found the white, blank wall too spotless.
There it stood, inviting, like a sheet of drawing paper. They quickly bought spray cans of paint and set about creating the really 'living' wall.
Those who had talent and those who had none at all sprayed the wall with the most fantastic colours: glaring green, riotous red, smudgy blue and yellow. The respectable man resented it. He had his wall whitewashed all over again and restored to immaculacy.
For the amused kids, who had nothing to do anyway, this temptation was too much, and so the story of the living wall repeats itself season after season.
Every day the wall changes from the most naive direct painting into a fanciful, abstract picture.
This living wall is the antipode of the well organized walls we find around our buildings.
The citizens of Amsterdam have long been confronted with the caricatures on the wall around Heineken's brewery.
Organized art should be confined within spaces that allow us to devote part of our attention to art.
Our own living room may be such a space, but also a room in a museum or a park with a wall or a sculpture.
In spaces like these we can really concentrate on works of art; let us leave other walls to youth and to the emotions.

Museum Journaal 4, Netherlands; 1966

These days many words are spoken about exhibitions, exhibition design and other related subjects. During the past 15 years I have been intimately involved in mounting exhibitions based on IDEAS, and I have always tried to emphasize the translation of the IDEA while planning the exhibition.
Too many exhibitons are made around a subject or the work of an artist by people with nothing more than a good basic knowledge of the subject and well-intentioned thoughts about the work of the artist. I am very often struck by the fact that curators of museums do not appear to care the slightest about the public who will see their exhibits. Both curators and officials are so involved, personally, with the work or the subject they are showing that they often forget that the public too must understand the idea behind the exhibition.
While trying to translate ideas into exhibitions I have always tried to bear the following in mind: the degree of willingness of the public to have the subject of the exhibition introduced to them, and the ability of the public to understand the exhibition.
To take the first point, the willingness of the public to go to an exhibition. Today it is very easy to gather a large audience for any exhibition which has a social movement as its theme. The involvement of the young people all over the world with social reform is well known. But, especially today, it would be worthwhile to encourage that other part of the audience – namely the older generation – to go to these exhibitions. In particular, those who have made up their minds that they do not wish to understand what young people of today are thinking. This is one of the most important, and at the same time one of the most difficult problems facing exhibition makers (and indeed communicators in other fields). Somehow we must discover a method of introducing the subject on display to our audience in the most easily understandable way. I fully realize that one of the most important tasks, not only of the exhibition makers but also of the exhibition announcers, is to inform the unwilling spectator of what he should be able to find in the exhibition. The announcement can be well designed and beautiful, but in addition it should always point out to the reluctant member of the audience what he personally might find, what he might 'get out of it'. There are still many adults who feel that they do not have anything more to learn, who think that their education finished when they left school, that they are now grown up and know enough about life, who have their ready-formed opinions and stick to them. They forget that the world is still turning, that movements come into existence and then disappear, that new truths become apparent every day because of the changing situation, not only in the arts but in science and world history. The education of these people should be our main target. The people who think they possess all the knowledge they need. These people should be drawn into our exhibitions and shown in the most simple way what it is all about.
To consider the other factor: the ability of the public to understand the exhibition. The method of approaching the public is very important. For each audience there is a method and it is very helpful if one knows what sort of public makes up the audience and what their interests are. The most difficult case is when the subject on exhibition is a general one and one is attempting to attract a wide and varied public. In that case the exhibition should be planned to appeal to the audience on different levels. The first level will explain the subject in its most broad and simple terms; the second level will go deeper into many elements of the subject; on the third level the specialist will have a chance to study details of the subject. Exhibitions should be planned taking these three levels into consideration so that the public can choose how much of the subject they wish to see depending on their knowledge and interest. Another point which designers for exhibitions should consider when their exhibit forms part of a larger exhibition, for example a trade fair, is that their display should be planned to harmonize with surrounding exhibits and not to compete with them. If designers can cooperate with each other when the exhibition is in its planning stage, a coordinated scheme will enable each exhibit to receive the attention it deserves, and will facilitate the spectators' understanding.

Part of a paper delivered at the International Symposium on Exhibition Design, IIIrd Biennale of Graphic Design, Brno, Czechoslovakia; June 19-22, 1969

Pieter Brattinga: Mediator, Han van der Meer.

... Brattinga's ebullient creativity of old seems to have found its proper channel today. 'I'm a translator, communicating the ideas and wishes of boards and individual clients to the group of artists. I've taken up a position between those two groups.' ... 'Seeing an interest in pure science without an application is ridiculous. You can't let that go. It's a shame when a scientist's work is left untranslated. Look for instance at the inexplicable case of Oppenheimer. A man of science who after so many years says: My God, what have I been doing? And society which then denounces him as a commie. It's beyond me, it's impossible really. The gap that's fixed between technologists on the one hand and the rest of humanity on the other. And also between technicians individually. They tuck themselves away in stifling backyards'.

The sigma idea is right up Brattinga's alley; he has a seat on the board of the Amsterdam Sigma Foundation. The latest sigma stunt was a street organ concert given in Dam Square. Still: 'This sigma thing can have a function. People must be kept sane, else they'l go to pieces through overspecialization. Every specialist can spend some of his time on other things. We all have time to spare; in fact, more and more of it'.

'The trade unions have failed, and I think the fault is all theirs. They've achieved a great deal, but they've neglected to think ahead. When in 1935-1938 the unions and socialist parties were setting down their basic ideas, they omitted to offer people something beyond mere material betterment. Mental progress, that's what is needed'. 'Even now, a fridge and a car are the signs that you've made it in life. Not the fact that you're a superb angler or a crack football player. And why not, may one ask?'

And also: 'A nation of football watchers is still a long way from being a nation of football players. The point is that we must learn to watch creatively instead of just watching creativeness. When you walk in the street you discover magnificent things, daft things. Little words, sewage lids, signboards'.

It appears that Brattinga is now using the almost chaotic complex of activities in a new, Renaissance-like profession, that of the forward thinking mediator between seemingly chaotic creativeness and overspecialized rationality. Between those who give assignments and those who receive them, between industrialists and designers. We can benefit. If only there were more Brattingas.

'De Volkskrant', Amsterdam, Netherlands; September 23rd, 1967

Exhibition 'Artypo' in the Stedelijk van Abbemuseum, Eindhoven
Graphic techniques as a basis for autonomous art, Ferd op de Coul

The graphic techniques used here have served as a means, as an element in creating the art work shown.
A single letter, printing ink, a silk screen, a block or a plate have played the role of foundation or component.
The exhibition comprises work by artists from Japan, the U.S.A., Germany, France, the Netherlands and England. It offers a richly varied picture of what can be accomplished with the help of graphic techniques. Items: Polke Sigmar's 'Strand '66', a screen block in black and white, enlarged – as it were – to gigantic proportions, oil on canvas. Very playful instances of 'concrete poetry', i.e. the meaning of the text is reflected in the letter and word image itself. Also superb 'circular scripts' by Ferdinand Kriwet, in which a given text is presented in different type characters arranged concentrically, like an old tree's annual rings.
Matthias Goeritz' relief print 'The golden message' is a graphic play on the word 'oro'.
Thus there are numerous specimens of graphic mastery and inventiveness.

'Eindhovens Dagblad', Eindhoven, Netherlands; March 11th, 1967

Goeritz, Matthias

Bense, Max

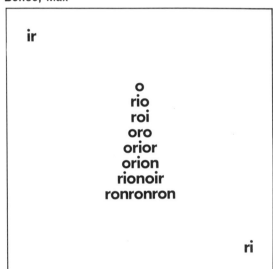

Kriwet, Ferdinand

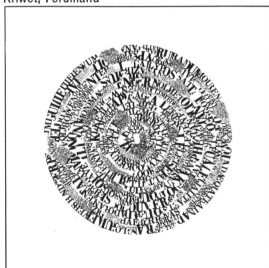

Begeer, Jan

Exhibition 'Form and Industrial Waste' in the Stedelijk Museum, Amsterdam
Incident shows whimsical forms in Stedelijk, Hans van Straten

Interest for the incidental and waste forms is not new, which does not mean that it is a very nice
idea to set up an exhibition with the name 'Form and Industrial Waste'. This is Brattinga's idea
and it is realized in the Stedelijk Museum of Amsterdam, new wing, main floor.
At the iron foundry the designers found strange forms in iron, at Lips and Philips, punched metal
plates and vegetable tins compressed into blocks. From Leerdam they brought complicated pieces
of glass.
Everything is very nice, they really did their best to bring together everything which has fascinating
form. In the iron pieces one can see everything one wants to see. These rusty pieces of metal look
like growth from an underworld, which has previously been unknown to us but now seems very
near.

'Het Vrije Volk', Amsterdam, Netherlands; 1959

Why is Industrial Waste exhibited in the Stedelijk Museum?

If some questions in the city council meetings are sometimes very unclear, one question is very direct: 'Are the Mayor and Aldermen of Amsterdam convinced that it is proper for the Stedelijk Museum to exhibit industrial waste in comparison with works of art using the same materials which are bought regularly using the taxpayers' money and exhibited?'
The Mayor and Aldermen answer that the exhibition 'Form and Industrial Waste' (they really do understand what the inquirer meant), intends 'to show by comparison the difference between art form and incidental form'.

'Het Parool', Amsterdam, Netherlands; 1959

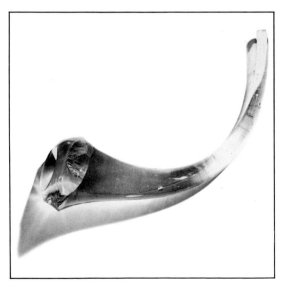

Mural in the Stedelijk Museum

The picture on the right shows a mural by Brattinga for an exhibition at the Stedelijk Museum in Amsterdam. It is designed to make a wall which develops from left to right. Although the different figures are in separate squares it will be seen that they share a similarity. They are, in fact, made with the help of the basic forms of a typeface. The typefaces 'T' and 'O' for example are clearly recognizable. In some instances a change in form is developed by double printing and a playful element comes into the entire composition. As every panel is interchangeable an enormous number of permutations in form is possible.

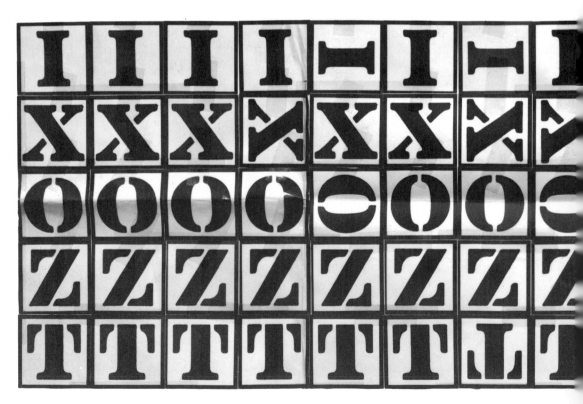

166

conway.

167

Posters for the Kröller-Müller Museum

The illustrations below and on the right show a number of posters which Brattinga designed for the Kröller-Müller Museum near Arnhem in the Netherlands. The Museum uses two or three designers of whom Brattinga is one.
It is not the Museum's policy to make use of an identifiable element in every poster, but although the Museum does not wish to have a recognizable style of its own, Brattinga has made a number of posters which not only show the exhibited subject clearly, but also succeed in giving the impression of the atmosphere of the Kröller-Müller Museum.
His knowledge of technique in general enabled Brattinga to develop a number of interesting posters without using very expensive reproduction techniques.

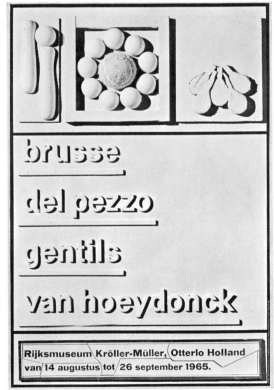

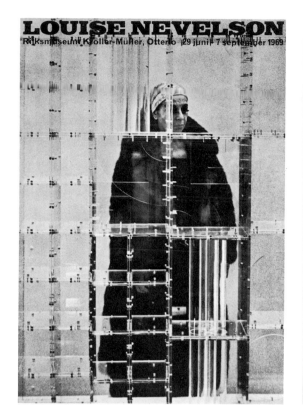

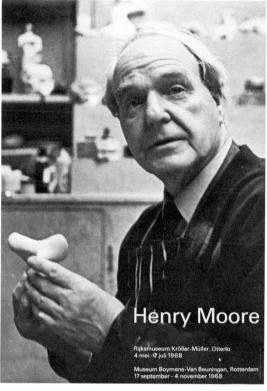

Planning for education

An educational programme for Pratt Institute

After Brattinga had been invited to lecture at Pratt Institute in 1960 he was asked to accept the appointment of Chairman of the Advertising Department of the Art School in 1961. Further observations on the training of designers followed most systematically after this appointment. Professor Brattinga spent a year researching and evaluating the programme being followed at Pratt and other American and European design and art institutes. His findings resulted in a proposal for a new educational programme for his department at Pratt Institute, which you will find in the form of a graph on this and the following four pages. After the acceptance of the new educational programme by the trustees of Pratt Institute, Mr. David Gates, who had lent much support in the developing and clarifying of many of Brattinga's ideas, became programme co-ordinator and, subsequently, after Professor Brattinga's departure from the U.S., Chairman of the department. With the introduction of this new educational programme Professor Brattinga published a preamble to the graphs on the following pages. It is divided into three short statements:

1. The Visual Communication Designer

The facet which is most important to the designer is his thinking. He must have a flexible and well-organized mind to enable him to:
1. Distinguish the real truth in a blurred and coloured presentation.
2. Abstract its essential points.
3. Translate these points, in their order of importance, into a coherent solution. It is quite possible, in fact, that if he is able to make a very clear summarized statement about his commission he will have solved half his problem.
The visual communication designer must have a knowledge of related fields as well as of the major developments in science, art and philosophy. Only if he has the ability to select those items of information from which he can draw his own conclusions will he be the right person to give form to communication between people. Unlike the fine artist, most concerned with expressing his own inner feelings, the visual communication designer is primarily an intermediary in the communication of ideas. His education, therefore, must enable him to understand the language of scientists, artists and officials, so that he can translate their thoughts and ideas into visual terms.
Specialization is one of the aspects of the visual communication field. Whereas the commercial artist of the twenties was his own illustrator, letterer and typographic designer, the designer of today usually occupies himself with only one segment of a project. Or while functioning as an art director, he must be able to engage and coordinate the services of other specialists for specific tasks. The designer of today very rarely makes an end product. His sketch, script or layout, unlike the autographic production of the fine artist, is only a plan for technical realization. He must develop his plan, therefore, within the limitations of a specific technical process.

2. Circumstances which shaped the Educational Programme for the Department of Advertising Design & Visual Communication.

While developing my ideas for the educational programme, I had to base my thoughts on:
1. The needs of industry and institutions in the field.
2. The ability and attitude of the student.
3. The teaching ability of a technically specialized faculty.
4. The sources available for education and training.
5. The possibilities of the future in the field of visual communication.

1. The needs of industry and institutions in the field of visual communication –
The educational environment should not be one of idealistic isolation; it must be based upon the present and future needs of the field, with the atmosphere, discipline and urgency of reality. The educational programme must be flexible enough to continually reflect the changes in modern communication.
2. The ability and attitude of the student –
With few exceptions, the student of today does not participate in community affairs, does not have any interest in fields other than his own, and does only that amount of research which is pointedly asked of him.

171

This might be the result of a number of social and economic factors, but it is also the result of unrealistic motivation in his early education, which does not develop the necessary self-discipline in the student. He continues to expect someone to furnish him with knowledge, skill and direction with the least effort on his own behalf. Therefore, a programme of higher education should be designed in such a way that good self-discipline is a major requirement.

3. The teaching ability of a technically specialized faculty –
To teach effectively, part-time instructors must constantly be aware of their contribution to the general plan of the programme. It is necessary to have an educator in the department who will co-ordinate the instruction of these highly valuable technical specialists.

4. The sources available for education and training –
The location of Pratt Institute, only 30 minutes from the cultural information sources and technical facilities of New York City, is one of the most ideal in the world for the student of visual communication.

5. The possibilities of the future in the field of visual communication –
Many programmes train with only the situation of today in mind. It is necessary, however, that we adjust our planning to the future needs and standards of communication. At the same time, of course, we must also furnish the student with the necessary knowledge and craftsmanship for today's requirements.

3. The Educational Programme of the Department of Advertising Design & Visual Communication.

The aim
The Programme is designed not only to provide the student with the necessary skill and knowledge for a good position in the field of visual communication, but also to prepare him for the future needs and possibilities of the field.

The Programme Content
The Programme, previously limited to the printed media area of advertising design, has now been expanded to include all facets of visual communication. The curriculum, leading to a degree of Bachelor of Fine Arts, is divided into four categories: Design for the Printed Media, Moviemaking, Photography and Television.

These technical subjects are supplemented by interdepartmental courses in drawing, painting and sculpture, and also courses in English language and literature, social studies and psychology.

A weekly design forum, conducted by visiting specialists, will include lectures on architecture, industrial design, graphic design, music, writing, painting, ethics in advertising, industrial practices and other subjects that will broaden the student's interest and knowledge.

The First Year
As a freshman in the Art School, the student attends classes in the Department of Foundation Art. There he receives fundamental training in the broad, underlying concepts of two and three dimensional form and colour. At the end of this year, the student will elect to specialize in one of the departments in the Pratt Institute Art School. Departments include: Advertising Design & Visual Communication, Art Education, Graphic Art or Industrial Design.

The Second Year
(in the Department of Advertising Design & Visual Communication)
In his sophomore year the student, while developing his craftsmanship, will concentrate on the history, theory and technology of the four main technical subjects: Design for Printed Media, Moviemaking, Photography and Television. He will also learn to develop his ideas in words by an exposure to copy, script and editorial writing, and will attend the following classes in the General Studies Department: Survey and Principles of Art, Social and Economic Institutions and Physical Education. Drawing, Painting and Sculpture courses will be given by the departments that specialize in these subjects.

The Third Year
In his Junior year, the student will be prepared to apply his acquired knowledge to creative problems in Design for Printed Media, Moviemaking, Photography and Television. At this time, rather than having one instructor for the full year in each subject, the student will be exposed to the developed knowledge of various specialists in the field. Each of the specialists will propose and control a project (or series of projects) that involves his own particular specialization. General Studies courses are: Late Nineteenth century Art, Contemporary Art, Impact of Science and Contemporary Civilization. Interdepartmental courses will be given in Drawing, Painting and Sculpture.

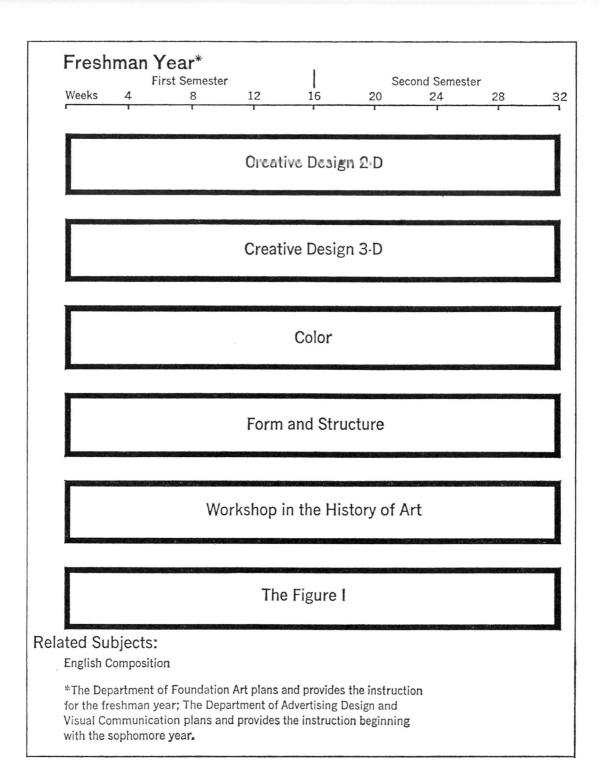

Freshman Year*

First Semester | Second Semester

Weeks 4 8 12 16 20 24 28 32

Creative Design 2-D

Creative Design 3-D

Color

Form and Structure

Workshop in the History of Art

The Figure I

Related Subjects:

English Composition

*The Department of Foundation Art plans and provides the instruction
for the freshman year; The Department of Advertising Design and
Visual Communication plans and provides the instruction beginning
with the sophomore year.

The Fourth Year
In his senior year, the student will work on a thesis project that involves one of the four main technical subjects: Design for the Printed Media, Moviemaking, Photography or Television. Although he will continue to attend classes in Drawing, Painting, and Sculpture, Psychology of Personality, Social Psychology and Great Books, he will be otherwise free to spend the major part of his time in developing a project that will indicate his craftsmanship as well as his thoughts and ideas, subject to the approval of an advisory board of faculty members and professionals. The student will meet with this advisory board throughout the year for guidance and criticism.

Visiting Committee
To maintain a programme that reflects the discipline and urgency of professional activity, a visiting committee of respected specialists will meet periodically to make evaluations and recommendations.

The reader will have noticed that the graph depicting the education in the sophomore year states subjects like: 'Landmarks of film', 'History of letter form', 'History of photography' and 'History of typographic design'.
The reason for the teaching, at this early stage, of the history of these specialized subjects results from Professor Brattinga's belief that a subject can be taught best if the student will accept the subject not as an axiom, but grow, together with his first exercises on the subject, with the subject.
This also explains teaching in: 'Specialized Tools', 'Type Workshop', 'Camera Work' and 'Photo Processing'. The history, together with acquiring technical or tool discipline, like the preceding subjects, will give the student a feeling that he does not simply have to accept certain facts his faculty teaches him but that he can follow the developments of the specialization.
Even though Professor Brattinga, whose background lies in industry and art, introduced these basic ideas in 1961, many art and design institutes all over the world will only allow the history of design subjects to be taught as a very last detail of a general course in History of Art and consequently teach students those necessary design subjects in their very last year of study.

Sophomore Year

	First Semester				Second Semester		
Weeks	4	8	12	16	20	24	28	32

Television I

Techniques	Production	Programming
Field Trips		

Film I

Cinematography	Editing	Special Effects	Principles of Animation	Sound
Landmarks of Film		Film Workshop		

Printed Media I

Principles of Design			
Specialized Tools	Print-making	Technical Realization Processes	Color Psychology
History of Letterform	Technique of Lettering	History of Typographic Design and Type Workshop	

Photography I

Camera Work	Photo Processing	Photo Lab
History of Photography	Practical Photographic Theory	

Drawing, Painting and Sculpture

The Figure II	
Painting I	Sculpture I

Related Subjects:

History of Design
Survey and Principles of Art I
Social Institutions
Economic Institutions
Design Forum I

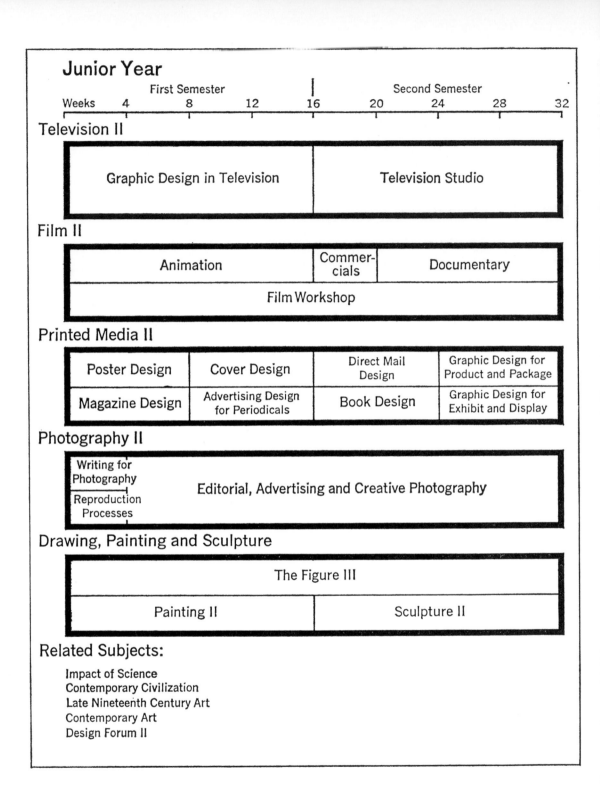

Junior Year

First Semester		Second Semester

Weeks   4   8   12   16   20   24   28   32

Television II

Graphic Design in Television	Television Studio

Film II

Animation	Commer-cials	Documentary
Film Workshop		

Printed Media II

Poster Design	Cover Design	Direct Mail Design	Graphic Design for Product and Package
Magazine Design	Advertising Design for Periodicals	Book Design	Graphic Design for Exhibit and Display

Photography II

Writing for Photography / Reproduction Processes	Editorial, Advertising and Creative Photography

Drawing, Painting and Sculpture

The Figure III	
Painting II	Sculpture II

Related Subjects:

Impact of Science
Contemporary Civilization
Late Nineteenth Century Art
Contemporary Art
Design Forum II

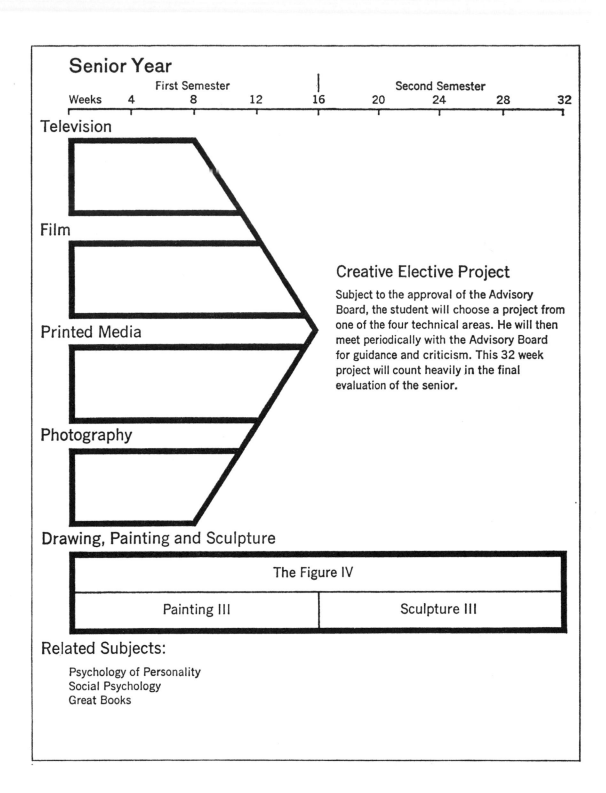

Senior Year

First Semester | Second Semester

Weeks   4   8   12   16   20   24   28   32

Television

Film

Printed Media

Creative Elective Project

Subject to the approval of the Advisory Board, the student will choose a project from one of the four technical areas. He will then meet periodically with the Advisory Board for guidance and criticism. This 32 week project will count heavily in the final evaluation of the senior.

Photography

Drawing, Painting and Sculpture

The Figure IV	
Painting III	Sculpture III

Related Subjects:

Psychology of Personality
Social Psychology
Great Books

Evaluation of an Art Academy, Pieter Brattinga

Although this report was commissioned by a specific Art Academy the requirements and recommendations in it could be adapted to fit many other Academies of Art.
After accepting your assignment to X-ray the Academy I have devoted the first few weeks to probing the general atmosphere prevailing in the various departments. Also I have looked for possible distinct signs of unrest after the former Director's departure. It was reassuring to find that the situation did not immediately call for any drastic changes.
Furthermore, during this first period I have defined the assignment clearly for myself on the basis of the facts you laid before me and taking account of the state of things as I found it to be.
My assignment could be divided into three distinct parts, as follows:
I.   Finding a suitable candidate for the post of Director.
II. Making suggestions for the curriculum within the rules set down by the Education Minister.
III. Providing co-ordination between municipal officers, Academy and architect with a view to possible building plans and the future situation at the Academy (as mentioned sub. II).
Before going into detail I would inform you that I have documented myself on each of the three points with various authorities and private persons from whom I received all possible cooperation.

Introduction

. . . I should like to dwell briefly on he purpose of the Academy as an educational institution. It is the task of the Academy to provide society with a number of young men and women who may be, or may become, valuable artists or designers. Helping to form the character of the young student when as a teenager he is admitted to the Academy is a major aspect of that task. Training the student to become an individual with a developed conscience and sense of responsibility as well as a good craftsman with a thorough grasp of his chosen discipline is a matter of the most vital importance to society at large. This is why, in my view, the character-building aspect of education should dominate all others.
The second important aspect of the educational task is to impart to the student the methods and techniques that will enable him in doing his work to employ his skill to the best advantage, rather than to be hampered by a lack of 'knowhow'. Hitherto the imparting or implanting of technical knowledge has constituted the burden of curricula in schools of art. The previously mentioned facet and the one I shall touch upon below have hardly ever received much attention.
In the third place, then, the educational institution must prepare the student for the normal needs of day-to-day business intercourse. Society is entitled to expect a graduate to be capable of writing intelligible letters, making phone calls and reading contracts. The difference between the education of the fine artist and the applied artist or designer, both of which trends are represented at the Academy, today constitutes a difficult problem when it comes to achieving proper co-ordination of the curriculum And no doubt it will grow even more difficult in the future with the expected progress of specialization. in the applied arts. For the sake of completeness I will clarify the difference between the two groups of creative specialists. The fine artist – the man who does not necessarily do work on assignment – will always strive to make his work express his emotions as faithfully as possible. He will make an effort to deliver work that is an entity in itself and by this entity add something new to the world's inventory. He will endeavour to approximate his feelings as closely as he can whilst – sometimes – he may proceed from the assumption that those who contemplate his work will be influenced by it (an influence which the artist may or may not regard as identical with what induced him to start creating his work). The techniques which the artist has learned to handle during his training period and which he has perfected after graduation will be entirely at his command in transmitting the emotions that have driven him to produce a given work of art.
The applied artist – the man who works exclusively by assignment – will endeavour to comply with all facets of what he has been asked to do in preparing his manufacturing plan, integrating form and colour into the essential demands, made so as to arrive at a complete, satisfactory solution.
In order to be able to work out his project effectively the applied artist or designer must learn to think clearly and analytically during his training years. He must be able to separate essentials from non-essentials in studying his commission and where necessary he must be able to add suggestions and considerations on elements not specified by the client. Furthermore he must learn to translate all the separate elements into a technically sound plan that satisfies the demands of economy and feasibility.

I. Finding a suitable candidate for the post of director. At this point I would like to revert to the first part of my own assignment, namely: finding a suitable candidate for the post of director. To solve the problem I have attempted to formulate a range of requirements that should be imposed on the person appointed.

1. The director shall refrain from giving excessive attention to one particular branch of his institution.
2. The director shall be capable of managing the administration and faculty of his institution as if he were heading a normal commercial enterprise.
3. The director shall be capable of giving guidance to his department heads and of co-ordinating the activities of the various departments.
4. If a dispute arises between a department head and a teacher, or between a teacher and a student, the director shall be capable of acting as a wise mediator.
5. The director shall be capable of implementing the wishes of the governors within the institution.
6. The director shall practise one form of art himself.
7. The director shall represent both the governors and the academy at meetings with the representative of the Ministry and other authorities.
8. The director shall represent the Academy at any manifestations organized by the Municipality.
9. The director shall have such a position within the city of X that he can secure aid on the part of municipal authorities whenever necessary.
10. The director shall be, and keep himself, informed of the latest developments in the fields of art, design and pedagogy to the extent of being able to incorporate them into his curriculum.
Although these demands are certainly not excessive or out of the ordinary I do not believe any of the candidates that have applied for the post so far fully meets the requirements listed.
Also in my view, the Academy, which is among the largest in the country, should be directed by a person who is permanently available on the premises.

II. Giving suggestions for the curriculum within the rules set down by the Education Minister.

I would now turn to the second part of my task, that of giving suggestions for the curriculum within the framework of the law.
As you know, the A commission set up by the Minister of Education, is making efforts to formulate a general programme for the teaching of arts and crafts.
It is likely that this programme, which comes within the new Educational Act, will be accepted by the Minister before September 1965.
What has transpired so far about the programme involved leads me to expect that my suggestions regarding your curriculum will not be at variance with the future possibilities as provided by the Act.
One of the principal considerations in adapting a new curriculum to the suggestions given by the A commission and creating a new situation at the Academy is the necessity of finding 'consumers' for the product delivered. I am using the term consumer on purpose in order to make it perfectly plain that the graduated students will have to find suitable jobs. Of course this requirement is most explicit in the case of the applied arts. Therefore, leaving aside the fine arts for a moment, we must ask ourselves whether there are good opportunities in and around X for such students. I have attempted to gather facts and figures on jobs held by graduates but unfortunately this proves to be impossible. I have had reports, unverifiable for the moment, to the effect that the majority of graduates have in fact found work in or around X. Thus with a view to the future of the Academy it is important to know what will be the future of X. The present efforts made by the city to create opportunities for more industrial enterprises to build plants at the M is indicative of the city's hope to become an ever more important centre of trade and commerce in Western Europe.

III. Providing co-ordination between municipal officers, Academy and architect with a view to possible building plans and the future situation at the Academy.

This brings me to the last part of my assignment – providing co-ordination between municipal officers, Academy and architect with a view to possible building plans of the Academy.
The very valuable plan to combine the various art schools into one Comprehensive Academy to be built in X has my full sympathy and support. The creation of a meeting place where the artistic disciplines are constantly confronted with one another may have a highly stimulating effect on the students.

With the plans for a large building, or complex of buildings, for such a Comprehensive Academy In mind I have studied the proposed site as well as the ex sting buildings at K and N.

Providing instruction at University level imposes certain requirements on the building used for the purpose, and these requirements, of course, should be basic to the blueprints prepared. For example, when inspecting the building at N, I was struck by the fact that the needs of education and architecture have been effectively co-ordinated so that the largest and heaviest materials and equipment are arranged on the ground floor.

At X all departments are accommodated in a group of single storey pavilion type buildings.

If the Comprehensive Academy should in effect be built on the site earmarked by the City Planning Department, a certain amount of high rise building would be indispensable. This implies that a larger or smaller proportion of the workshops with their heavy machinery would have to be housed on one floor. I do not know how far this will interfere with the need for tranquillity and good acoustics in the spaces reserved for the schools of music, drama and the dance.

Furthermore, some of the vibration developed by the machinery employed may be a nuisance for the music department.

Also I have studied the problem of transportation of materials (stone, concrete, paper, musical instruments, scenery etc.). On the strength of the above considerations I have arrived at the following conclusions:

A very considerable time will go into merely establishing the basic needs of all schools housed in the Academy. On the other hand, the Academy cannot wait much longer for a new building. I would suggest therefore, that a different project from the one initially made by the city of X be adopted. Since some 8000 square metres will be required for the Academy alone, whereas the site suggested does not measure more than 4000 square metres, a large multistoried building would be called for. In view of the drawbacks described I propose that Academy (or Comprehensive Academy) be constructed on a different site and on the pavilion principle.

This is what I have in mind:

A central, permanent main building comprising a janitor's lodge, a large hall for film, dance, music, lectures, etc., a library, a hall providing opportunity for some 50 students to study or listen to records, sound tracks or educational films individually, an exhibition hall, a cafeteria and a number of rooms for director(s) and administration.

Secondly, a number of pavilions grouped around the main building and based on the number of schools in the Academy or Comprehensive Academy.

Each pavilion providing accommodation for a workshop, halls and rooms. The pavilion should be equipped with movable walls to permit changes of space in conformity with requirements imposed by given projects and by the education provided in a given term.

The reason why I should like to introduce the plan in question not only lies in the fact that I fear the adoption of a single large building will give a great many difficulties, but also that education is likely to undergo considerable change in the next fifteen years. The progressive development of various manufacturing techniques is certainly going to affect the content of the instruction given and workshops will have to be adapted in a way that cannot be predicted as yet.

I would recommend, therefore, that the cost of building the pavilions be restricted to the extent of giving them an almost semi-permanent character as the popular term is. The point is that it should be possible for the individual pavilions to be reconstructed or renovated in ten-year periods, in accordance with the evolving demands of education. On the other hand, the administration building should be permanent and calculated to serve for a very long time.

I would add a further remark on the cafeteria to be located in the main building. At the universities in the United States it is usual for a cafeteria to be leased by a catering organization. Management and price level are established in consultation with the university's administrative department.

I would propose a similar system, taking into account the probability that the exhibitions and performances to be held in the building will draw a large public so that there would be adequate grounds for projecting an auditorium in the space reserved for the cafeteria.

A report, 1965

180

Elements of consideration for the training of the visual communication designer, Pieter Brattinga

It's very important that we first establish exactly who is a designer. During the last week I have listened to many specialists on the Jury and it was quite clear to me that when we were talking about a designer we were all talking about something different. And so I'd like to offer a suggestion and some statements on the definition of a designer.

Nowadays a designer is consulted by his clients. A designer listens to his clients like a physician listens to a patient. And a designer has to 'take' from a very long complicated story. (It is never a straightforward story which the client gives the designer). The designer's task is to select from this large story all the elementary points in order of their importance. He should be able to take out of this presentation some very clear statements. This analysis is one of the most important steps that a designer has to take.

I very often find that when we are talking about an artist or a designer that the two are often confused. An artist, if he wants to make or create something according to the feelings in his heart, will make a creation that need not be limited or stimulated by rational analysis. Because he is his own client and his feelings are more important than the factual points which are given by the client. The only thing which I find that the artist and designer have in common is, to some extent, responsibility towards society.

Especially today, in the 60s, when we have seen so many developments in the political, in the moral and in many other aspects of life, the artist and designer alike have a moral responsibility towards society. And, of course, we can see great examples of this moral responsibility already in the 1920s, after World War I, when new ideas in art and design started in Europe.

Another point of difference between an artist and a designer is that the designer's work, the sketch which he makes in his studio, is not the end but only the beginning; while for the artist, the work that leaves his studio is the end, a final product. It's because of this, therefore, that I sometimes hesitate to judge or discuss sketches of posters. Because they are not end products. They are only the beginning of something which still has to be created. They are like the plan of an architect or a technical drawing. Another point is that the designer has to have some knowledge of the production-line. Since I am here in Warsaw, I might make this comparison to the Polish posters. To my great surprise I have always found that the magnificent Polish posters are reproduced from finished sketches and that they are never produced in cooperation with the printer.

The beautiful sketch for a poster-to-be could be produced on a lithographic stone or a zincplate. They could be produced by the artist himself. But I don't think it is fair to the Polish poster to have the sketch reproduced instead of being produced, because I am quite certain that if the designer himself works with the technician at the printing-works, the end result will be at least twenty times better. I therefore think that it is most important for the designer to have some technical knowledge of printing. He should know what methods of printing are available, when to use one kind of printing technique and when to use another. This is important because it will shape the design before anything is put down on paper.

Now another subject is skill in business practices. I found to my surprise that many of my students did not know how to handle a telephone, they were frightened by it and they said the most rude things on the telephone. They didn't know how to write a letter, how to put anything on paper. They didn't know how to talk. This holding the telephone and talking in a polite manner, this business talk, this writing a letter is also part of the profession of a designer. A designer should not be a man wearing a dirty sweater or with dirty hands. He is a professional man. Like a physician, he is a member of an honoured profession and he should be treated as a professional. This also means that he should be able to talk on the telephone and be polite, be civilized.

I went to the United States in 1960, and in 1961 I was asked to change the educational programme of my department at Pratt Institute. I did a lot of research and I went to industry to find out what should be taught and to what extent design graduates from the school can be employed in industry. To my surprise I found that in most cases industrial organizations have a two-year programme to re-train the designer.

Therefore, I based my programme on these industrial requirements. But not the requirements of today, these are unimportant, no, the requirements of five years from now are much more important.

There was something else I found: in the U.S. specialization in certain fields goes so far, that specialists only know their own limited field. This is dangerous because different specialists have nothing in common, no poetry, no knowledge about films, no theatre, nothing!

Only a specialized field

You remember the great example of the case of Dr. Oppenheimer, the atomic scientist who used his moral judgment and was looked upon as a traitor. Specialization without knowledge of other disciplines is the most dangerous, and I think that it might sometimes be the cause of many of the misunderstandings in the world today, and even of wars.

Our designers should know about the new movements in poetry, what is happening in music, what is electric music, what is concrete music, what is new in the theatre, what is ballet, what's happening in architecture. This is one of the old rules we can learn from the Bauhaus. I don't want to speak about the Bauhaus now, but there are many things which we could learn from older institutions.

Besides, when a designer becomes an Art Director he has to have a wide range of knowledge. When a designer has to do a job for the medical world he has to know what is of interest to doctors, what is the latest in medical research. A designer today has to read many magazines and papers.

The working method of a designer could be very simple. He should talk about the 'why', 'who', 'where', 'when', and lastly – and it's very important because somebody has to pay – 'how much'. Now if the designer is working along these lines, very directly, very hard, very precisely, whenever he finds an answer for the 'why', 'what', 'how', 'when' or 'where', he should go back to it and try to understand what the answer is and how he has arrived at it.

And, if a designer can do this, he will have solved half the problems involved. The education of a designer. I developed a new educational programme for my department at Pratt. I found that the system which is used in many parts of the world is still very much like the old beaux arts system. A student goes to a master and the master eventually gives him a very small commission. This is a very old procedure: Rembrandt had students like that, Rubens too. But this cannot be the method any longer. Each individual that comes to our schools, has to be stimulated. We don't have to put a stamp on him, we have to do it by a method which is designed to expose the student to different elements of visual communication. And I am using the words Visual Communication because I think that in the future we are not going to talk about graphic design, but visual communication. Visual Communication is television, film, photography, and design for the printed media.

My educational programme is divided into five equal parts: a day each for film, photography, design for the printed media, painting and sculpture. These days young people cannot absorb English literature, history of art, economics and other subjects all in one day. To give you an example: this programme will have one day each week devoted solely to television. In the morning one aspect of television will be under scrutiny, in the afternoon, another aspect. But, for the entire day the mind will be on television. The next day the subject will be photography, and so on for the rest of the week.

For the technical subjects I wanted to adopt a different approach. I started by taking a camera apart to show how the camera works, what goes on inside, what happens when you develop a film. Later in the same day one of my instructors was teaching the history of photography. What the first photographer discovered.

And why this way? Because I found to my amazement that in most European and American schools the history of art is not studied until the last year of education, and suddenly the student hears about Man Ray in Paris making photograms, Rayograms.

This is so wrong because we should start with the subject together with its own history. So I developed these points and I started a course called the History of Design, which started with the subject after the Industrial Revolution.

This way I tried to build a system which, although simple, is, I think, very logical. During the final year the student is required to specialize in one of the four technical subjects – film, photography, design for the printed media or television – and a commission from industry is arranged for the student. The commission is unpaid but is controlled by the industry to ensure that the design received is what was required. At the same time the school sees that the student does not bypass what he has learnt previously.

All of us remember the day we left school. We didn't know anything, we had to go out and find a job. Nobody helped us. We couldn't go back because we were so afraid. After three months when we had our first job we tried to ask our former teacher a question, but we couldn't get back into school, so we had to make our own decision.

Publ. 'Documentation des débats du symposium organisé à l'occasion de la Ie Biennale Internationale de l'Affiche, Varsovie 1966'.

Appendix

Biographical Chronology

1931	Born January 31st at Hilversum, the Netherlands.
1946	After interrupted studies during the war, enrolled at the International Quakerschool at Castle Eerde.
1949/50	Studies History of Art, Drawing and Painting and Printing techniques in Paris, Leyden and London.
1952	Joins the printing firm steendrukkerij de Jong & Co in Hilversum, Netherlands.
1954	Establishes an Art Gallery for steendrukkerij de Jong & Co. From the opening statement: '. . . in order to genuinely support the arts we will never show any work of sponsors . . .'
1955	Starts publishing and editing the 'Quadrat Prints' for steendrukkerij de Jong & Co.
1957	The 'Pictura Prize' of the Royal Academy of The Hague is awarded to steendrukkerij de Jong & Co. From the citation: '. . . Through these exhibitions the public and your workers get acquainted with the best examples of international art, while your non-commercial publications the Quadrat Prints, are of a perfect typographic design and high literary standard'.
1958/61	Member of the Art Council of the Municipality of Hilversum.
1958/present	Advises a number of industries, museums and institutions on art and design.
1959	Coordinates the meetings and activities of a new group of industrial designers, the '7'. (later N.I.D.F.)
1959	Invited by Sandberg, realizes his ideas for an exhibition 'Form and Industrial Wastes' (now considered a forerunner of 'junk art') in the Stedelijk Museum of Amsterdam.
1960	The museum of Modern Art in New York adds two of his designs to her collection and exhibits them in her exhibition 'Recent Acquisitions'.
1960	Member of the graphic designers organisation Gkf.
1960	Invited by Pratt Institute to lecture on typographic design during the academic year 1960-1961.
1961	Invited by the Yale University School of Art and Architecture to give a lecture about design for steendrukkerij de Jong & Co.
1961	Holds a seminar at the Southern Illinois University on the use of the form of typeface.
1961	Appointed Professor of Art at Pratt Institute.
1961	Appointed Chairman of the department of Advertising Design and Visual Communication of Pratt Institute.
1961	Studies educational programmes of design schools in the U.S., Germany, Switzerland and the Netherlands. Develops a new educational programme for Pratt Institute with equal emphasis on television, photography, film making and design for printing.
1962	Travels for three months through Canada, Western U.S., Mexico and Southern U.S..
1962	His work as director of design for steendrukkerij de Jong & Co, is shown in a section of the exhibition 'Design for Industry' in the Stedelijk Museum in Amsterdam. (Other shown industries: Geigy of Basel and the Container Corporation of America).
1963	Gives his slide lecture 'Communication in the street' at 'La casa del Libro' in San Juan, Puerto Rico.
1963	Lectures on 'Communication in the Street' at the Minneapolis School of Art.
1963	Gives a lecture series on the pioneer Piet Zwart at the Yale University, School of Art and Architecture, during the academic year 1963-1964.
1963	His section of the exhibition 'Design for Industry' is shown at many musea throughout Europe: The Hague; Ghent and Tongeren, Belgium; Linz, Austria.
1964	Silver medal Triennale of Milan.

1964	Makes a lecture tour to Los Angeles (U.C.L.A.), Hawaii (A.A. Chapter) Tokyo (Kuwazawa Design School, Tokyo Art Directors Club), Osaka (Naniwa University), Hongkong, Saigon, Djakarta, Bangkok, New Delhi (Indian Cultural Institute), Cairo, Jeruzalem, Tel Aviv, Athens, Beograd, Zürich, Amsterdam.
1964	Establishes in Amsterdam the office of Form Mediation, International.
1964	Chairman of a panel discussion on design education at the first congress of Icograda in Zürich, Switzerland.
1964	Member of the ICSID working group on 'Doctrine and Definition'.
1964	Two of his posters are shown at the exhibition 'The photographic Poster' at the Museum of Modern Art in New York.
1965	Lectures at the Naniwa University in Osaka, Japan for four weeks.
1965	Consultant to the VARA Broadcasting Corporation in regard to the design of their Radio-T.V. Guide.
1965	Lectures for the A.G.W. in Stuttgart, Germany on 'the Education of the Designer'.
1965	Co-opted member of the Board of Icograda.
1965	Makes, with Wim Schippers in his series of exhibitions, a 'programme of smells' which receives world-wide attention.
1965/68	President of the Art Directors Club Nederland.
1965	Founding of an experimental printshop 'Typotent' in Amsterdam.
1965	Lectures in New Delhi and in Chandigarh at several schools of architecture and design.
1966	Gives a lecture on 'genuine support of the arts' at the Institute of Contemporary Arts I.C.A. in London.
1966	Presides a forum in the Stedelijk Museum, Amsterdam on the subject 'Experiment, why?'.
1966	Member of the jury for the awards of Dutch Advertising Design of 1965.
1966	An exhibition of his posters and those of Dick Bruna is opened in New Delhi by the Governor of Jammu and Kashmir State, Dr. Karan Singh.
1966	Opens exhibition 'Design for steendrukkerij de Jong & Co' in the Landes-Gewerbe Amt in Stuttgart.
1966	Opens an exhibition of the work of Indiana in the Stedelijk van Abbe-museum, Eindhoven, with a transmitted interview with the painter.
1966	Member of an international jury to award prizes in the International Biennale of the Poster in Warsaw.
1966	Lectures on the education of the graphic designer at the symposium at the I International Biennale of the Poster in Warsaw.
1966	Member of the board of the Netherlands Art Foundation, castle Zeist, Netherlands.
1966	Elected secretary general of the International Council of Societies of Graphic Design Icograda during the general assembly of Icograda in Bled, Yougoslavia.
1966	Consultant to the Dutch State Mines, D.S.M..
1966	Member of the board of the Sigma Centre, Amsterdam.
1966	Gives a series of lectures in Kansas City, Kansas City Art Institute St. Louis, Washington University; Chicago, I.I.T.; New York, Pratt Institute and Parsons School of Design.
1967	Directs, with Frans van Mastricht, and participates in a radio documentary on education in applied arts.
1967	Chairman of the jury and organizer of the exhibition Artypo (art made with the help of graphic techniques) at the Stedelijk van Abbemuseum, Eindhoven.
1967	Organizes and directs, with Thijs Chanowski, a session of the National Advertising Congress in the Netherlands on the 'Possibilities of the Future', aspects in communication by smelling, feeling, seeing and hearing.

1967	Makes with his wife, a writer, a study-tour to the Middle East, Iran, Pakistan, India, Thailand, Vietnam, Hongkong, Japan, Hawaii, the U.S..
1968	The Museum of Modern Art, New York, shows three of his designs in the exhibition 'Word and Image'.
1968	Designer of the catalogue for Carel Visser, the Dutch participant in the Biennale of Venice.
1968	Makes a radio documentary on the opening of the Biennale of Venice and the Dokumenta in Kassel.
1968	Receives the Grand Prize from the Jury of the International Survey of Exhibition Design in the Third Biennale of Graphic Arts at Brno, Czechoslovakia.
1968	Supervises the preparation of the third General Assembly of the International Council of Societies of Graphic Design Association in Eindhoven.
1968	Re-elected unanimously as Secretary General of Icograda.
1968	Introduces as President of the Art Directors Club Nederland the first published survey of visual communication in the Netherlands, in an 'Art Directors Annual'.
1968	Co-authors 'A history of the Dutch Poster 1890-1960' with Dick Dooyes.
1969	Member of the acquisition committee for the collection of contemporary art of the town Utrecht.
1969	Lectures at a number of Art Schools and Universities in Groningen, Twenthe, Eindhoven and Nijmegen on visual communication, art and technology and perception.
1969	Designs special postage stamp to commemorate the fifteenth anniversary of the Statute for the Kingdom of the Netherlands. (Surinam and the Antilles).

Writings by Pieter Brattinga in the following media:

Winkler Prins Encyclopedia, a statement on Graphic Art and Applied Graphic Art, 1960
Het 'Drukkersweekblad', Netherlands, general articles, since 1960
'Magnum' Germany, an article on the 'Style of the Future', 1961
'Haarlems Dagblad' Netherlands daily, an article on the responsibility of the editors: 'All the news that's fit to print', 1961
'Catalogue, Gene Feldman' Stedelijk Museum, Amsterdam, an introduction, 1962
'Typography 62' a catalogue of the society of Typographic Designers of Canada, an appreciation, 1962
'Print' U.S., an article on a 'Common Design Language' 1962
'Artists Proof' U.S., an article on Gene Feldman, 1962
'Pagina' Italy, an article on Gene Feldman, 1963
'Packaging design' U.S., an article 'The third world of international Packaging', 1963
'Photography' England, an article 'The relationship Photography/Typography', 1963
'Ariadne' Netherlands, a general series on advertising since 1963
'Gebrauchsgraphik' Germany, a general series on design, since 1963
'Industrial Design in the Netherlands' Walker Art Center, Minneapolis, U.S.A., a brochure, 1964
'Industriële Vormgeving in Nederland' Museum Journaal, Netherlands, a brochure, 1964
'Piet Zwart' Prins Bernhard Fonds, Netherlands, a pictorial essay, 1964
'Graphic Design' Japan, an article 'Werkman and Feldman', 1964
'Design' India, an article on graphic design, 1965
'Museum Journaal' Netherlands, an article on the 'living wall and fence', no 4, 1966
Catalogue Artypo, Stedelijk van Abbemuseum, Eindhoven,
'Artypo in the 20th century, an article on art made with the help of graphic techniques, 1967
'A history of the Dutch Poster' co-author Dick Dooyes, 154 pages, publ.: Scheltema and Holkema, Amsterdam 1968, a book.

Between 1960 and 1964, Pieter Brattinga has taped a number of interviews with leading personalities in the arts at the Voice of America for re-broadcasting in the Netherlands. Among them were: Edward Steichen, Karel Appel, Len Lye, Joop Sanders, Shinkichi Tajiri, Will Sandberg, William Seitz, Jan van der Marck, Saul Bass, Wim Rietveld and Robert Indiana.
Since 1967 he taped interviews with Drs. Eberhard and Phylis Kronhausen, Dr. D. Mahlo, Ad Dekkers, Jos Manders, Pierre Restany, Dr. J. Leering, Michael Kustow, Dr. Medkowa, Ferenc Horvath, Bill Kluver, John Weber, Henry Moore, Jacob Landau, Arman, Ad Petersen, Olaf Leu, Waldemar Swierzy, Stanislav Kovar, Prof. Josef Svoboda.

Brattinga's designs are published in most of the well known international annuals and publications and are in the possession of the Library of Congress, Washington D.C., The Kunstgewerbe Museum, Zürich, The Stedelijk Museum, Amsterdam, Wilanow Palace, Department of the National Museum, Warsaw and many other museums.

Writings about Brattinga
illustrated articles:

Walter Plata in 'Form und Technik' number 12, Germany 1960
Bernard Majorick in 'Typografia' number 2, England 1960
Hans Kuh in 'Gebrauchsgraphik' number 12, Germany 1960
Dr. Karl Pawek in 'Magnum' number 31, Germany 1960
Hiroshi Ohchi in 'Idea' number 43, Japan 1960
Katsumi Masaru in 'Graphic Design' number 6, Japan 1962
Katsumi Masaki in 'Graphic Design' number 8, Japan 1962
Wil Sandberg in 'Catalogue Number 321' of the Stedelijk Museum, Amsterdam 1962
Johan H. van Eikeren in 'Tete' number 5, Netherlands 1962
Richard Janssen in 'Ariadne' number 22, Netherlands 1963
Opland in 'Graphis' number 115, Switzerland 1964
The editors of 'Newsweek' September 20, U.S.A. 1965
The editors of 'Der Spiegel' September 29, Germany 1965
The editors of 'Print' number 2, U.S.A. 1965
Kho Liang Ie in 'Domus' number 423, Italy 1965
Belle Bruins in 'De vrouw en haar huis' number 5, Netherlands 1966
The art critics of 'the Statesman', 'the Hindustan Times', 'The Patriot' and 'the Times of India' of April 11th, India 1966
T. de Klerk in 'Eindhovens Dagblad' August 5, Netherlands 1966
J. van Duinhoven in 'Het Algemeen Dagblad', March 15, Netherlands 1967
The editor of 'Trouw', July 8th, Netherlands 1967
F. H. K. Henrion and Alan Parkin in 'Design coordination and corporate Image' publ.: Studio Vista, London; Reinhold Publishing Corporation, New York (pages 200 through 207) Fall 1967
Han van der Meer in 'de Volkskrant', September 23rd, Netherlands 1967
Louwrien Wijers, 'Algemeen Handelsblad', February 13th, Netherlands 1968
Liddy van Marissing, 'de Volkskrant', August 9th, Netherlands 1968
Lambert Tegenbosch, 'de Volkskrant', August 17th, Netherlands 1968
Mildred Constantine, Ed and Allan M. Fern in 'Word and Image', publ.: The Museum of Modern Art, New York, U.S.A. (page 96 and 110) 1969

Notes

1) Page 18
The committee consisted of:
DSM, Information Service:
P. Frische
M. Verjans
G. Pattijn
J. Vonk
W. Simons
H. Haane
H. Zeekaf
J. Slothouber
W. Graatsma
DSM, Printing Department:
H. Reijnen
DSM, Administration Department of Organisation:
K. Steenwijk
DSM, Patent Department:
J. Andriesma

2) Page 24
Headed by Brattinga, the design team consisted of: Ph. van Meeuwen and Evert van den Brink

3) Page 24
Presently the radio-tv guide is visually created by: Werner Paans, art director and Evert van den Brink, with Brattinga acting as consultant.

Register of names

Reviewers, art critics and authors

Brattinga-Kooy, Willemijn, 118, 124
Constantine, Mildred, 47
Coul, Ferd op de, 162
Doelman, C., 152
Dooyes, Dick, 18, 138, 144
Fern, Alan M., 47
Henrion, F. H. K., 31, 113
Herdeg, Walter, 30
Horst, H. van der, 128
Katsumi, Masaki, 28, 30
Keulen, Jan van, 146
Koenraads, Jan P., 126
Marissing, Lidy van, 15
Meer, Han van der,
Moran, James, 128
Opland, 32
Parkin, Alan, 31, 113
Ramaker, Theo, 130
Redeker, Hans, 134
Reichardt, Jasia, 40
Sandberg, W., 113, 134
Schulze Vellinghausen, Albert, 116, 124
Stankowski, Anton, 31
Straten, Hans van, 165
Tegenbosch, Lambert, 44, 142
Uemura, Tokachiyo, 34
Vinkenoog, Simon, 13
Visser, M., 118

Other executing artists, designers and architects

Bons, Jan, 41, 133
Boxsel, Pim van, 43
Chagall, Marc, 33
Crouwel, Wim, 43, 117, 127, 129, 131, 137, 139, 145
Jongejans, Charles, 121
Katavolos, William, 37
Kho, Liang, Ie, 117, 125, 127, 135
Miller, Henri, 43
Munari, Bruno, 35
Raateland, Ton, 35, 41
Rietveld, G., 39
Rot, Diter, 41
Sandberg, W., 33,45
Sierman, Harry, 35
Tajiri, 123
Treumann, Otto, 33
Wernars, Gerard, 127, 129, 131, 135, 137, 142, 147, 149
Wissing, Benno, 140